# Preface

I'm ashamed to admit it now, but when I think back to my many holidays in North Devon, the Lake District and Wales in the seventies and eighties, when the sight of Hunters in pairs, pairs of pairs, or just solo was so normal, I can recall thinking 'Where's the RAF's modern stuff?' They were there of course – just never enough to satisfy me. I dare to admit that I had become bored by the appearance of these superannuated Hunters (but better them than Gnats!) 'Heresy' – I can hear the cry.

Hopefully readers might forgive my early sins and keep me from the Inquisition's less than tender mercies – but it does make me wonder: was I the only one to think like that?

P.S – don't blame Neil, I didn't even know him in those days. I'm afraid this passage relates solely to the errant 'other chap'!

As with earlier books in this series, to labour a point, Neil and I do not pretend that this work represents a full development, service, or operational history of the Hunter: how could it when the space simply isn't available? Moreover, several lengthy books have appeared across the years which have attempted to cover those very aspects, with, no doubt, other complete histories due in the future.

Thus, as ever, we aim this book squarely at the modeller, the nostalgist and the enthusiast with, hopefully, sufficient background information to place the Hunter in context.

Now, a plea: in order to gain from this book, the authors would urge the reader to explore the appendices and notes provided at the back _first_!

### Authors' notes
Excluding prototypes, photographs are arranged by unit in ascending numerical order with squadrons first, then OCUs, followed by other training and subsidiary units. Initial consideration was given to arranging them by serial number, however, given the long service lives of so many Hunters, whether in original or converted form, the result was an unstructured muddle and the thought was discarded.

Known in full, officially, as Hawker Siddeley Aircraft Ltd since 1935, the company reformed its aviation interests in 1948 to become the Hawker Siddeley Group, a division of which later became Hawker Siddeley Aviation responsible for aircraft design. This arrangement survived until 1977 when the Labour Government enforced the merging of Hawker Siddeley Aviation, Hawker Siddeley Dynamics, Scottish Aviation and the British Aircraft Corporation to form British Aerospace.

Given the quantity of Hunter airframes that were later to be reacquired by the manufacturer for conversion to other Marks, bought back for spares recovery, overhaul or resale, it is sometimes expedient to use the abbreviation HSA when referring to the manufacturer. For the record, however, the familiar prefix 'Hawker' was applied to the company's post-war aircraft designs until c1963 when their products were rebranded to become Hawker Siddeley or HS – thus HS Kestrel, HS Harrier etc.

### Acknowledgements
The authors would like to express their sincere thanks and gratitude to Chris Ayre, Ray Ball, Tony Buttler, Fred Martin, Huw Morgan, Bill Newton, Terry Patrick, Andy Scott and Mike Verier for their much-appreciated assistance with this book. Equally, we gratefully acknowledge the always-generous help provided by Mike Smith (Curator of the Newark Air Museum) and his colleague Mick Coombes. Of course, we could not have managed without the continued assistance of Mark Gauntlett who, beyond supplying such excellent colour illustrations, also provided us with a great deal of extra assistance with regard to some of the lesser known aspects of the iconic, but confusing, Hunter. Mark, the time is surely approaching when you should consider writing the definitive 'Hunter Story'... Neil and I know of a pretty good illustrator!

Atmosphere. There's plenty of it to inhale here! Hunters fitted with 100-series Avon engines used a cartridge starter holding three cartridges (each about the size of a 2-pdr shell casing) indexed automatically for each start. In addition to making a distinctive sound, the start-up produced a lot of smoke as can be seen. Hunters fitted with 200-series engines used an AVPIN starter similar to that found on Lightnings. AVPIN (Iso Propyl Nitrate) is volatile, it burns without oxygen and produces hydrocyanic acid gas and photos exist showing groundcrew lurking under the Hunter's starter exhaust with an asbestos glove ready to beat out any lingering flames during start-up: apparently berets would be used as an alternative! _Photo courtesy of Terry Patrick_

# Introduction

One of Britain's classic post-war jet interceptor aircraft, the Hawker Hunter F.1 entered RAF service in July 1954. In later years it matured significantly to become a successful fighter-bomber, a fighter-reconnaissance aircraft, and (suitably modified), an exceptional two-seat trainer used by the RAF, FAA and RAE.

Widely exported, new and reconditioned Hunters represented a commercial success story spanning many years, while in Britain reconditioned and upgraded airframes continued in use for decades, albeit in ever-diminishing numbers, until, finally, the last Hunter to operate with the British military, T.7, XL612 (operated by the ETPS) made its final flight on 10 August 2001. Even the most cold-hearted bureaucrat would surely concede, in the final analysis, that the Hunter really didn't owe the British tax payer much.

The first British designed single-seat, swept-wing, high-speed subsonic day fighter to enter widespread service with the RAF, the Hunter replaced RAF Fighter Command's existing day fighters, the Gloster Meteor F.8 and Canadair Sabre F.4 in Britain, as well as replacing RAF DH Venoms and ten squadrons of Sabre F.4s in West Germany.

Five Marks of new-build single-seat Hunters entered RAF service at home and abroad: The F.1, F.2, F.4, F.5 and F.6. The new interceptor's performance transformed the RAF's day fighter squadrons from the mid-1950s, despite being initially plagued by a number of problems which included compressor stalls when firing the guns. Although the Armstrong Siddeley Sapphire-engined variants (F.2 and F.5) did not suffer from as many problems as the early Rolls-Royce Avon-powered Hunters, and enjoyed slightly better fuel economy, Sapphire-powered Hunters did experience several engine failures which led the RAF to persevere with the Avon in order to simplify long-term supply and maintenance issues given that the Avon was also used by the Canberra bomber. But, beyond such concerns there also loomed another, that perennial scourge of so many British-designed interceptors – lack of range!

Eventually nearly all the issues and faults were overcome, assisted in no small way by the allocation of perhaps twenty early production F.1s for use as virtual prototypes. The Hunter programme had allowed for a mere three actual prototypes – a parsimonious, not to say ludicrous quantity for such an important aircraft at a time when the UK would find it difficult to counter the Soviet Tu-4 'Bull' strategic bomber by day (let alone by night). Worse yet, reports of a new Soviet jet fighter were confirmed when the MiG-15 burst onto the scene over northern Korea to the consternation of Western democracies. (Happily, the same error would not be repeated with the English Electric Lightning. *See Flight Craft 11*)

Fortunately, the Hunter would prove to be a success in its primary role as a day fighter, with successive Marks serving with numerous frontline RAF squadrons throughout the second half of the 1950s. Enhancing its day-fighter capabilities was the provision of a gun-laying radar for the four nose-mounted 30mm Aden (Armament Development ENfield) Mk.4 revolver cannon with a *cyclic* rate of 1,300 rounds per gun per minute. Seemingly anachronistic today, the Adens offered almost unparalleled aerial firepower in a pre-air-to-air missile era. The guns were mounted in a detachable ventral gun-pack that contained the breeches of the four cannon and their ammunition, allowing the pack to be quickly removed on landing and replaced with a pre-loaded unit – the cannon barrels remaining in the aircraft while the pack itself was changed. This allowed for a rapid rearming and turnaround time which was further improved on later Hunters by the inclusion of a single-point pressure-input refuelling system. Such features allowed the Hunter to be readied between sorties in just seven or eight minutes if required.

In retrospect it now seems odd to consider that by mid-1960 the RAF had introduced the Lightning F.1 into squadron service and the replacement of the Hunter F.6 as the premier interceptor had begun, such was the pace of development in the 1950s and the strategic threats which had to be countered. Yet, as history records, the Hunter FGA.9 would remain in use as a ground attack aircraft until 1971, beyond which it and several other Marks would be utilized for training and subsidiary roles until the last Hunter was finally discharged in 2001.

**Opposite page:** Hawker P.1067, WB188; the first Hunter prototype and the forerunner of all subsequent Marks. First flown on 20 July 1951, WB188 was 'equipped' with nose ballast in lieu of four 30mm Aden cannon following delays created by the Ministry of Supply (MoS) who argued for the 20mm Hispano stating, among other concerns that the provision of four Aden cannon would make the airframe too nose heavy. In retrospect it appears that their primary concern was simply one of cost!

From the same sequence as the previous image taken circa (c) September 1951, WB188 displays its undersides to advantage and reveals the absence of airbrakes and cannon. At this time WB188 was painted using a bespoke overall colour, by HSA, which has since been described as 'glossy Duck Egg Green', 'pale Duck Egg Green', and 'a pale form of Sky' by various observers. *Both: Tony Buttler collection*

# Early Days

Used for ongoing research, WB188 was destined to become, in the form seen here, the sole Hunter F.3. In this image taken prior to its successful attempt on the world air speed record (727.6 mph on 7 September 1953), WB188 – by now painted red, had received a sharply pointed nose, afterburning Avon RA.7R engine, new jet nozzle, and a pair of clam-shell airbrakes with distinctive hinges and hydraulic rams mounted on the rear fuselage. Later, in the quest for greater speed, various airframe protrusions were removed including the rams and hinges mentioned, as were the airbrakes – each cavity then being skinned over. A new streamlined front canopy of increased rake was also fitted, albeit after this photo was taken. *Tony Buttler collection*

Today WB188 will be familiar to most readers in its preserved F.3 form as seen here at Greenham Common in July 1976. Following its world air speed record success WB188 was soon retired, receiving maintenance serial number 7154M on 10.11.54. Since September 1992 the airframe has been on loan to the Tangmere Military Aviation Museum where, in 2018, it still resides. *Fred Martin collection*

WB195, the second prototype Hunter, first flew in May 1952 wearing the same colour scheme as WB188 on its initial flight. WB195 differed in several respects, not least of which was the provision of a working Aden gun pack and associated gun-ranging radar. WB195's flying life was also short and in September 1955 it became 7284M. Thereafter it survived until sold for scrap in December 1967. *via Fred Martin*

# Hunter F.1 and F.2

Hunter F.1, WT594, seen during a pre-delivery flight in mid-1954. This image amply illustrates its clean lines; only the 'bolt-on' ventral airbrake disturbs the symmetry, enforcing the perception of it being the afterthought that it was. It did, though, finally provide the answer to one of the Hunter's most intractable problems – how to decelerate quickly under certain conditions of flight. Other solutions had been sought, including the use of perforated split flaps, landing flaps, and WB188's clam-shell installation – all of which created additional handling problems or insufficient deceleration or both. Of the many faults revealed by F.1s, early examples did at least serve to help solve this problem which led to the fitting of a ventral airbrake as standard. *Newark Air Museum*

The Hunter F.1 powered by the Rolls-Royce Avon 113 was the initial production model and first flew on 16 May 1953. Of the 139 built the first twenty or so were seconded for development purposes. The F.2, of which 45 were built, was powered by the Armstrong Siddeley Sapphire 101 engine and first flew on 14 October 1953.

The new fighter soon revealed a number of serious problems, not least being the lack of a true airbrake, pilots instead relying on their wing flaps, a poor substitute given the latter were incapable of slowing the superbly streamlined interceptor down rapidly under certain conditions of flight. Consequently, a simple hinged airbrake was developed and scabbed onto the underside of the aft fuselage of those airframes still on the production line or already stored pending the modification prior to being released to operational squadrons – the first being 43 Squadron which received F.1s in July 1954, followed by 257 Squadron (F.2s) two months later.

Another difficulty soon encountered by F.1 pilots was engine surge, something the Sapphire-powered F.2 did not suffer from. A surge could occur under various flight conditions, but the surge most commonly recalled was the one created when the guns were fired and their gases were ingested into the engine. Until a satisfactory solution was found, the rather unsatisfactory

Hunter F.1, WT594 'U', as seen later in 1955 while serving with 43 Squadron. The latter became the first squadron to introduce the Hunter into operational RAF service in July 1954, retaining them until late 1956 (albeit supplanted by F.4s from February 1956). Points of interest include the retrofitted link collectors or 'Sabrinas' to WT622 'G'; the 'low' positioning of the unit's black and white fuselage chequers and the short-lived placing of individual code letters under the tailplane. Tail cones could be swapped from one airframe to another, as appears to have occurred on WT622 – hence the code letter might also have to be reapplied too. *Tony Buttler collection*

temporary 'solution' was to reduce fuel flow to the engine when firing the cannon, which other than causing a significant loss of thrust, also restricted the F.1 to firing its guns at less than 25,000ft at a maximum speed not exceeding 275 mph.

Nonetheless, it was clear from the outset that the Hunter offered exceptional performance with considerable potential once these (and other) faults were resolved, one of which in particular demanded urgent attention.

Arguably the greatest flaw with the F.1 and F.2 was an abysmal lack of range which, earlier endurance-related accidents aside, was tragically demonstrated on 8 February 1956 when six Hunters were lost. Eight F.1s from the Day Fighter Leader School departed RAF West Raynham in Norfolk at 10.50am to carry out an exercise at 45,000 feet in the local area. Due to expected bad weather later in the day, the aircraft were scheduled to return to West Raynham by 11.15am, but by 11.00am the weather had deteriorated with poor visibility and the aircraft were told to divert to nearby RAF Marham for a visual approach. Visibility reduced further and due to the close proximity of the aircraft to each other it was not possible to complete Ground Controlled Approaches. In the following confusion, six aircraft were lost – (four pilots ejected after their fuel was exhausted, one pilot force landed following a flame-out just east of the airfield and one aircraft crashed northwest of Swaffham, killing the pilot) – only two aircraft landed successfully.

To address the problem, a production F.1 was fitted with modified wings featuring additional fuel tanks in the wing leading edges and 'wet' hardpoints for underwing tanks – which ultimately led to a change of designation to the Hunter F.4.

*Please refer to Appendix 1 for details of operational RAF Hunter squadrons and flights.*

**Opposite page:** Having equipped 43 and 222 Squadrons in 1954, 54 Squadron became the third and final operational F.1 unit in February 1955. It had been intended that 247 receive this Mark too, but they went to 54 Squadron instead. Seen wearing blue and yellow chequered bars on the nose either side of their lion motif, the checks would, at a later stage, be enlarged and their number reduced. WT659 'U' is nearest the camera with WW636 leading – the latter sporting what appears to be a yellow lightning flash across its blue upper fin and rudder, while the rearmost, WT692 'S', carries what appears to be a blue lightning flash, either over a slightly darker shade of yellow (to contrast with the unit's lighter yellow fin codes) or maybe even freshly applied Post Office Red (BS 381C 538) on its upper fin and rudder, perhaps indicating they were Flight Commanders' aircraft. Also of interest are the 'dark' wingtips, which were possibly blue – although identifying colours from b&w photos can never be an exact science. The fourth Hunter was WT696 'O' the latter sporting a yellow lightning flash across its fin and rudder, while the rearmost, WT692 'S' carries a blue flash on a Dark Sea Grey upper fin and rudder. The fourth Hunter was WT696 'O'. Fin codes were yellow and wingtips blue. Soon removed from front-line service, many F.1s were simply scrapped, but others joined those already serving with 229 and 233 OCU, AFDS and DFLS amongst other users. *Tony Buttler collection*

**Above:** Many F.1s were allocated for test, trials, research and development work for which just one example, WW605, must suffice. Delivered in September 1954 to 233 OCU, F.1, WW605, was later used variously by Rolls-Royce, the RAE and A&AEE and is seen here c1955 possibly employed on de-icing tests which could explain the rig beneath the Sabrina and ducting along the fuselage. Day-glo has been applied to the rear fuselage, nose and outer wings. *Tony Buttler collection*

**Below:** With de-icing equipment removed WW605 is seen at a later undisclosed date with reduced day-glo. This airframe spent its last few years serving as a wingless fuselage in a wind tunnel until finally being dumped at Farnborough in 1963. *Tony Buttler collection*

First flown on 30 November 1952 powered by an Armstrong Siddeley Sapphire engine, WB202 became the prototype Hunter F.2. Production F.2s (and subsequent F.5s) were all Sapphire powered in contrast to the Rolls-Royce Avon-powered Hunter F.1, F.4, F.6, T.7 and later derivatives. Finished in High Speed Silver overall and fitted with four cannon, WB202 was involved in gun trials from February 1953, following which it too joined the quest to solve the thorny problem of developing a suitable airbrake: a problem finally resolved in June 1954. Used also to investigate the aerodynamic qualities of (dummy) drop tanks in an early attempt to remedy the appalling lack of range inflicted upon the first Hunters, WB202 was ultimately SOC on 31 December 1957 and scrapped in 1960. *via Fred Martin*

Other than the single example received by 1 Squadron, the only operational units to receive the Hunter F.2 were 257 and 263 Squadrons at Wattisham in 1954 and 1955 respectively. In this image both aircraft display their 257 Squadron green and yellow chequers on the rear fuselage with individual code letters on the fin. The nearest Hunter, WN950 'F', clearly shows its yellow-painted nose door, although its black code letter is less evident. Delivered to 257 Squadron on 31 December 1954, WN950 was dispatched to 5MU, Kemble, in April 1957 and was sold as scrap in April 1958.
*Tony Buttler collection*

257 Squadron soon moved its chequered bars to the nose placed either side of their motif – the chinthe, a mythical lion-like creature, which faced forward on the starboard side and presumably did so on the port too! This image of F.2, WN907 'H' was taken c April 1957, probably after arrival at 5MU, but wherever it was, WN907 had been static for a while to judge by the locks on the flying control surfaces and the drooped airbrake and flaps caused by the slow release of hydraulic pressure.
*Authors' collection*

# Hunter F.4

F.4, XF990 'K', in 3 Squadron markings, was the Geilenkirchen Wing Leader's mount as confirmed by the pennant fronted by three vertically arranged emblems on the nose: one each for the Wing's constituent units namely; 2 (Swift FR.5s), 3 and 234 Squadrons. Because 3 Squadron, like so many German-based Hunter units, existed for months rather than years photos relating to them can prove to be scarce. Luckily, XF990 attended the Paris Air Show where this photo was taken in May 1957. A week or so later it was serving as 'ES-16' with 229 OCU. 3 Squadron's fuselage bars were solid green outlined in yellow, while the fin code was red outlined in white. XF990 survived to be sold to Switzerland in 1972 and was SOC in January 1992.
*Tony Buttler collection*

Reportedly, some early production F.4s retained the Avon 113 initially; if so it was soon succeeded by the Avon 115. Later, several F.4 airframes were upgraded to receive the Avon 121. The F.4 introduced the first large-scale revision to the Hunter F.1 production line, which included an increased internal fuel capacity from 334 gallons in the F.1 to 414 gallons in the F.4, to which 'wet' underwing hard points for 100-gal drop tanks were also provided (for both the F.4 and F.5, yet they were rarely used it would seem).

The first Hunter F.4 flew on 19 October 1954, while the first squadron to receive the Mark, by a small margin, was German-based 98 Squadron commencing 15 April 1955 at Jever.

Another teething problem encountered by all early Hunters included a tendency for ejected ammunition links to hit and damage the underside of the fuselage and ventral airbrake fairing. To remedy this, teardrop-shaped streamlined blisters were designed to fit over the ammunition link ejector chutes to collect the discarded links. Initially introduced on the F.4 and F.5, they were sometimes retrofitted to the F.1 and F.2 as well. Often referred to as 'Sabrinas', the name was synonymous with a well-endowed British film star of the period.

To deal with a similar problem caused by spent cannon cartridge cases, their original cartridge ejection chutes were simply extended to protrude into the airstream – thus helping to resolve that problem.

F.4, WV275 'D', from 4 Squadron, displaying the unit's bars either side of the fuselage roundel. The bars would ultimately be reduced in size and relocated to the nose either side of their motif. WV275 served with 4 Squadron from July 1955 to March 1957 when it went to 229 OCU.
*Fred Martin collection*

**Top:** F.4, XF299 'O', served only with 43 Squadron, following which it was sent to 5MU where this photo was taken in the late 1950s. Repurchased by HSA in August 1961, it was broken up for spares. By comparison to the unit's F.1s it may be seen that the individual code has been relocated from the aft fuselage to the fin, and the chequers raised slightly to the cleaner upper areas of the fuselage. In this view the white wingtips with small black checks may be seen, so too can the Squadron's fighting cock motif on the nose. *Tony Buttler collection*

**Right:** F.4, WV269 'H', 74 Squadron. Seen during Exercise *Vigilant* in May 1957, 74 Squadron's Hunters had sections of fin painted in a white distemper as an identity feature, with a panel left clear to avoid obscuring their yellow code letters. Delivered in June 1955, WV269 served until delivered to 5MU in late 1957 or early 1958 where it was scrapped in March 1961. *Newark Air Museum*

**Left:** Jever-based Hunter F.4s belonging to 93 Squadron accompanied by another from co-located 118 Squadron. WV277 'F' flies closest to the camera and was operated by the Squadron from January 1956 to April 1957. 93 Squadron's Hunters display their dark blue bars, outlined in yellow, containing stylised yellow arrows either side of the fuselage roundel. Barely visible sadly are the unit's nose markings – a blue disc thinly outlined in yellow containing a yellow heraldic emblem consisting of eight radiating spokes, four to form a basic cross and the others a saltire, with each spoke terminating in a fleur-de-lis. Fin code letters were applied in yellow and usually repeated on the nosewheel door in black. *Tony Buttler collection*

**Opposite, top:** With its fine lines undisturbed by cartridge link collectors, Jever-based F.4, WT802 'P', from 98 Squadron is seen in 1957. Unit markings are repeated on the nose either side of the Squadron badge bearing their motif Cerberus – the multi-headed hound of Hades. Although the unit survived until 25 July 1957, WT802 had arrived at 5MU by 9 July where it remained until declared NEA (non-effective airframe) on 7 October 1959. Bought by HSA, it was scrapped in 1964. *Fred Martin collection*

**Opposite, centre:** F.4, XE665 'A' was transferred to Jever-based 118 Squadron on 17 April 1956 and remained until June 1956. Returned to HSA, XE665 was converted to a T.8 and delivered to the FAA (Fleet Air Arm) in April 1959. Later, after a period in storage, it was transferred to the RAF in 1980 where it served with 237 OCU and 208 Squadron until transferred to the Fleet Requirements and Air Direction Unit in 1984. Returning to 1956, XE665 displays 118 Squadron's colours – alternating wavy white/black lines either side of the fuselage roundel repeated in miniature on the nose either side of the unit badge. The fin code was yellow, repeated in black on the nosewheel door. *Tony Buttler collection*

**Left:** Seen languishing at 5MU, F.4 XF298 'E', had arrived at Kemble on or about 21 May 1957 after serving with Brüggen-based 130 Squadron. The latter's markings remain in situ, including the elephant head motif superimposed on the Squadron colours on the nose: the fuselage serial number is missing. Sold to HSA on 8 September 1961, XE298 was broken up for spares at Baginton in late 1962. *Tony Buttler collection*

Also seen at Kemble following its arrival there in November 1957 is F.4, WV327 'U', late of 222 Squadron displaying its red and blue chequered bars. On 7 February 1961, WV237 became 7670M at 1 SoTT, Halton. Sold to HSA for spares recovery in 1975, 7670M was subsequently scrapped. *Tony Buttler collection*

A poor-quality image of Odiham-based 247 Squadron F.4, WV317 'S', seen between May 1955 and April 1957. The bars either side of the roundel were solid red thinly outlined in black, while the code 'S' was pale yellow thinly outlined in black – although it is barely discernible in this image. WV317 was sold as scrap at 5MU in March 1961. *Newark Air Museum*

F.4, XE675, as seen at Kemble c1960 following service with 229 OCU which it joined in April 1957. 229 OCU generally used codes 'ES' and 'RS' until about 1960 and usually applied them in white – but not here. Equally, individual code numbers were often painted white too, although here it is pale yellow. Red wingtips aside, the wings justify further comment too. Following the completion of about 100 'straight-wing' F.6s, leading-edge wing extensions were introduced on the F.6 production line to cure the type's tendency to pitch up under certain conditions of flight. Less often appreciated is the fact that small numbers of F.4s (XE675 was one), were also fitted retrospectively with the same extensions; perhaps they were intended for training units to ensure student pilots gained experience on aircraft as closely representative to those in use with frontline units as possible. *Tony Buttler collection*

F.4s were also used for experimental purposes of which WT703 was one. Seen here, it is believed, in 1956, it was being used extensively by the manufacturer for external stores clearance trials including various bombs, rockets, launchers and 100-gallon drop tanks. *Tony Buttler collection*

# Hunter F.5

The F.5 retained the Sapphire 101 engine used by the F.2, albeit some sources suggest it was modified to produce 8,300lb of thrust. The first F.5 flew on 20 October 1954 and featured a modified wing with fuel tanks in the leading edges and 'wet' hardpoints, essentially as per the F.4. Hunter F.5s entered service with 263 Squadron in April/May 1955 and became the first Hunter variant to see combat service during Operation *Musketeer* – the Suez Crisis of October/November 1956.

Seen in 1957, F.5 WP136 'N', belonging to 34 Squadron, displays its eye-catching unit markings in no uncertain manner. Placed in a purple-outlined arrowhead containing black and yellow chequers, a black wolf prowls in front of a yellow crescent moon on a white disc. The nosewheel door is black with a yellow 'N'. 34 Squadron also tended to paint their Hunter's nose caps – both black and white are known choices, but here it is neither, although the camouflage demarcation is lower than the rest of the fuselage indicating a replacement nose cap from another airframe. Both the F.5 and F.4 were fitted with underwing hardpoints and cleared to carry various stores as required, but they were rarely utilized by either Mark in service – making WP136 unusual in that it was photographed carrying 100-gallon drop tanks. *Authors' collection*

Doubtless the least flattering image of a Hunter to be found in this book, it does illustrate 41 Squadron's nose markings – a red double-armed cross thinly outlined in white, flanked by two white, red, white bars both thinly outlined in black. This is the carcass of F.5 WN972, previously 'U' of 41 Squadron, which was obtained by the MoS on 4 February 1959 and eventually ended up on the Farnborough dump where this photo was taken in 1964. *Tony Buttler collection*

56 Squadron Hunter F.5s in formation displaying their red and white chequered wingtips to advantage. Points of interest include the individual code letters on the nosewheel doors of WN979 'E' and WP103 'J' while that on WP104 is chequered. Note: WN979 appears to have had a substantial part of its starboard wing reskinned; WP103 carries underwing hardpoints (one per wing at mid-point); and they all have link collectors fitted. All three were flown to 49MU Colerne in November and December 1958 and were later sold to HSA for spares recovery.

F.5, WP120 'S', 56 Squadron, seen in May 1956 at Mildenhall. Despite appearances, the 'white' disc with the unit's phoenix superimposed is in fact pale blue. Following later service with 1 Squadron, WP120 was subsequently used in fatigue tests by HSA and tested to destruction.

F.5, WP186 was delivered to 5MU on 19 July 1955 and by August, was at Biggin Hill with the words 'Biggin Hill Stn Flt' on the nosewheel door (according to the hand-written note on the back of the photo). The pennant and the letters 'DGS' on the fin confirm that WP186 was, for a time, the personal mount of W/C Denis G Smallwood. By late 1958, after service with 56 Squadron, WP186 was at 49MU where it remained until declared NEA in March 1959. *All: Tony Buttler collection*

# Hunter F.6

The first F.6s entered service in July 1956 with 263 Squadron and was the first Hunter to be fitted with the Avon 203 which produced 10,000lb of thrust, an increase of about a third over the earlier Avons. The Avon 203 was an (almost) new design, fitted with a new compressor which put an end to surge problems, an annular combustion chamber, and an improved fuel control system. Other alterations introduced on the F.6 included a revised fuselage fuel tank layout and the introduction of four rubber tanks positioned ahead of the main spar in each wing, giving it an internal fuel capacity of 390 gallons (somewhat less than the F.4's internal capacity of 414 gallons). However, the F.6 was fitted with the Mod.228 four-pylon wing, initially trialled by an F.4, that allowed it to carry four 100 gallon drop tanks to much enhance its range.

To overcome 'pitch-up' problems when high 'g' forces were applied at high speed and at high altitudes, new and distinctive leading-edge extensions were applied to the outer wing sections which increased the wing area by nine square feet and often led to them being called 'sawtooth' or 'dogtooth' wings. The first hundred or so F.6s were completed without these extensions, although most had them fitted retrospectively.

A gun camera was installed in the nose, while the Ekco nose-mounted gun-laying radar provided automatic ranging for aiming various pylon-mounted weapons which could, if required, accommodate tiered 3in rocket projectiles, 68mm SNEB rockets in 18-round Matra pods, or 1,000lb bombs.

**Top:** Seen landing at Gütersloh, F.6, XJ642 'A' joined 14 Squadron on 8 April 1957. As can be seen the Squadron's distinctive white bars with blue diamonds were placed either side of the fuselage roundel in what we will call the 'low' position. The serial number is black as is the fin code on a white disc. Two Bristol 100-gallon finless plastic drop tanks are also visible – one per inboard pylon. Later converted to FGA.9 standard, XJ642 was sold to Singapore in May 1971. *Fred Martin collection*

**Above:** Operated by 14 Squadron from January 1961 to February 1962, this view of F.6, XJ636 'S', shows the final presentation of 14 Squadron's F.6 markings. Namely: the raising of the fuselage bars to a 'high' position (to avoid staining created by the engine cooling exhausts); white serial number and a white fin code on a black disc. The code letter was repeated in blue on a white nosewheel door, sometimes accompanied by three miniature diamonds below the code. Later converted to FGA.9 standard, XJ636 served until 25 October 1976 when it crashed at Mathry, Wales. *Tony Buttler collection*

F.6, XF449 'S', from 19 Squadron. Delivered to the unit at Church Fenton in 1957, this example displays a yellow fin code which was repeated in blue on the nosewheel door. XF449 was one of many 'straight wing' F.6s from the early production batches to be completed without leading-edge wing extensions (colloquially dubbed 'sawtooth' or 'dogtooth') which cured the Hunter's inclination to pitch up under certain conditions of flight. All surviving 'straight wing' F.6s later received the extensions including XF449. A leaking fuel valve caused this Hunter to catch fire while taxying at Binbrook on 6 June 1963: it was written off as a result. *Tony Buttler collection*

F.6, XG199 'J', 19 Squadron, 19 September 1961. Despite having been 'clipped' this image illustrates the changes made to the unit's markings by 1961 when compared to XF449. White wingtips with a thin blue lightning flash were introduced c early 1958, at which point the unit badge and miniature blue and white chequered bars were applied to the nose. At a later date the unit's fin codes were amended to white, as too were the serial numbers. *Author's collection*

Hunter F.6, XF417 'B' and F.6 XE530 'A', 26 Squadron, 1959. The unit markings include a springbok's (aft-facing) head on a white disc thinly outlined in a shade of reddish brown. The disc is flanked by two black bars thinly outlined in yellow with each containing a green lightning flash, the **pointed** end of which had been angled down and inwards on their F.4s, then reversed on the F.6 so that the point was directed upwards to the upper outer corners. The yellow fin codes, thinly outlined in green, were repeated using the same colours on the nosewheel door. *Tony Buttler collection*

XE530 showing the springbok head facing forward – i.e. facing forward port side, facing aft starboard side – plus green lightning flashes pointing up to the outer corners of each bar. What appears to be a Squadron Leader's pennant is carried under the windscreen. *Tony Buttler collection*

Photographed early in 1960, F.6, XF420 'K', from 54 Squadron reveals the changes made to the unit's blue and yellow checks which, in 1957, were reduced in number, increased in size, and had their sequence reversed compared to those applied to their F.1s which had twelve checks either side of the lion motif. The lion also became more prominent when it too was enlarged and placed on a white disc thinly outlined in blue. The fin code presentation seen here, a blue letter on a yellow disc, appears to have been a late change probably introduced shortly before the unit re-equipped with the FGA.9 in March 1960, many of which also used the same style fin code. Never converted, XF420 crashed on 27 July 1973 as a result of engine failure. *Author's collection*

An unidentified 56 Squadron Hunter displays its red and white chequered bars, thinly outlined in pale blue, either side of a yellow phoenix rising from a red fire on a pale blue disc. The nose cone, as so often seen in such photos, would appear to be a mismatched replacement. *Newark Air Museum*

F.6, XG159 'P', seen while operating with 56 Squadron who received it on 25 January 1960. Unit markings and wingtip colours remain much the same as per F.5 WP120 'S'. XG159 has gun-muzzle blast deflectors fitted. *Tony Buttler collection*

63 Squadron operated Hunters until it disbanded as an operational unit on 30 October 1958. However, the number was soon resurrected as a reserve squadron and as such continued to fly Hunters under the auspices of parent organisations such as CFS, 229 OCU and the TWU. On 2 September 1974, its title was formalised as 63(R) [i.e. Reserve] Squadron. (**Note**: in 1956 reserve units had briefly been termed shadow units, but a year or so later, 'shadow' was officially replaced by 'reserve'.) This photo of F.6, XF414 'P', taken on 20 September 1958, illustrates an operational 63 Squadron Hunter – its bold black and yellow chequers combining to virtually obscure similar checks on the wingtip. Note the raked fin code which was repeated on the nosewheel door in black. Converted to FGA.9 standard in 1961, XF414 was lost on 20 February 1967 as a result of engine failure. *Author's collection*

Previously operated by the DFLS, this worn, chipped and tired looking F.6, XG158 'O', from 65 Squadron reveals an unusual square 'patch' near its port wing root that coincides precisely with a skin panel. Was it a replacement panel, or had the paint been removed to check for damage perhaps? Used operationally only by 65 Squadron, XG158 went on to serve with several training units until 14 April 1981 when it became 8686M at Cranwell before moving to Farnborough in 1982. Thereafter, it went to the Pendine Ranges in Wales where it expired c1999. *Newark Air Museum*

F.6 'M', from 65 Squadron, displays its unit markings. Equipped with Hunters from December 1956 until March 1961, the F.6 was the only single-seat variant used prior to disbanding. The motif consists of a lion and fifteen swords, hilts to the ground, on a white disc. The addition of white bars made the red chevrons infinitely more visible than they had been when the unit flew Meteor F.8s. The Squadron's raked fin codes were yellow, as was the thinly outlined code on the cordite-stained nosewheel door. The gun-muzzle blast deflectors are particularly evident here. *Author's collection*

Delivered to the RAF on 1 February 1957, F.6, XF462 was later allocated to 66 Squadron. Quickly selected as the CO's mount and seen c1958, it was characterised by having a rattlesnake motif on the fin in lieu of a white code letter. In 1958, the Squadron altered the style of their markings from a motif flanked by two bars on the nose, to those seen here – a blue-bordered rear-facing white triangle bisected by the roundel, white wingtips, and a Squadron badge on a white disc on the nose. A few of their F.6s later received raked fin flashes, as did at least one T.7.
*Tony Buttler collection*

F.6, XG236, belonging to 66 Squadron offers a variation from the norm. Photographed prior to 7 May 1957, XG236 was being ferried to Iraq for the one-off purpose of acting as a backup for other aircraft taking part in a flypast over Baghdad on 7 May itself, for which purpose Iraqi markings had been applied, albeit while still retaining its RAF serial number and 66 Squadron fin code. Mission complete, XG236 returned to its unit at Acklington but was destroyed in a fatal crash at Kielder Forest on 14 February 1958. *Via author*

F.6, XE610 'J', from 74 Squadron, seen prior to receiving leading-edge wing extensions – adding to the impression that, other than introducing white wingtips, their F.6s looked little different from the F.4s they replaced. *Tony Buttler collection*

F.6, XG164 'H', from 74 Squadron. Delivered in 1956, this aircraft served with 111, 74 and 1 Squadrons, West Raynham Station Flight, 229 OCU, 4 FTS and the TWU before receiving the maintenance serial 8681M. Seen in its heyday, XG164 wears 74 Squadron's tiger face motif and bars on its nose and the code 'H' on the nosewheel door. *Tony Buttler collection*

Many readers will be familiar with the 92 Squadron trait of displaying yellow and red checks across the base of the fin on some of their F.6s, as well as either side of the motif on the nose. Seen in 1957/58, and as yet without white wingtips, F.6, XG234 'E' exhibits an earlier style motif combining a willowy full-length cobra and two red maple leaves painted directly onto the camouflage itself. The yellow fin code is repeated in black on the nosewheel door. Commencing August 1959, the Squadron motif was amended to incorporate a larger cobra head with a single maple leaf superimposed on a white disc. *Tony Buttler collection*

Called the '*Blue Diamonds*', 92 Squadron formed the RAF's official aerobatic team for the 1961-1962 season for which their Hunters received a special colour scheme of overall glossy Aircraft Blue with white cheat lines, wingtips and white-outlined roundels. Serials were black, as was the fin code above the fin flash while the code on the nosewheel door was white as seen here on F.6, XG137 'E'. *Tony Buttler collection*

Having received Hunter F.6s in November 1956, 111 Squadron formed the RAF's aerobatic team in 1957, for which, after considerable colour and pattern experimentation, overall glossy black was selected as the most suitable colour for their prestigious role and led to them being christened the *'Black Arrows'*. Here, F.6, XG203 is seen prior to 30 April 1957, the day it bounced while landing at North Weald, cartwheeled, broke up and caught fire. Astonishingly the pilot was involuntarily ejected sideways and survived. As a point of interest, most accounts state that *'Black Arrow'* roundels and fin flashes were bordered in white from the outset – but such was not the case with XG203, nor the Hunter behind it! Almost obliterated by the sun's glare, a small Union Flag is positioned below the front portion of canopy.
*Newark Air Museum*

'Black Arrow' XF506 'X', the mount of Sqn Ldr Latham is seen in October 1958 wearing 'Treble One' Squadron's heavily outlined black bars on either side of the Squadron badge, below the front canopy sill. The bars, pilot's name and rank insignia were carried on the port side only. Clearly, the roundels and fin flashes are outlined in white while the code letter 'X' is red, as too were the fuselage serial numbers, although they are not visible here. Underwing serials were dispensed with. *Tony Buttler collection*

Seen in 1958, F.6, XG168 'G-W' had been delivered to 208 Squadron on 20 March that year and became the mount of Sqn Ldr Granville-White, hence the rank insignia on the nose, and his personalized fin code applied in yellow thinly outlined with black. The bars, thinly outlined in black either side of the fuselage roundel, were pale blue and divided by a yellow stripe, the latter very thinly bordered also – possibly in black. Wingtips were white. Returned to HSA in August 1959, XG168 later re-emerged as an FR.10. *Tony Buttler collection*

On 1 July 1979, 216 Squadron reformed at Honington as the fourth UK-based RAF Buccaneer unit which also operated Hunter two-seaters in lieu of a dedicated Buccaneer trainer. On 4 July 1980 it relocated to Lossiemouth and was still in the process of becoming operational when the Buccaneer fleet was temporarily grounded. Consequently, the Hunter element was expanded to allow pilot training to continue, albeit not for long, as 216 was absorbed by 12 Squadron a month later. Seen here however, in July 1980, and only recently out of the paint shop is F.6, XF383, the only single-seat Hunter operated by 216 Squadron and which, uniquely, became the only single-seat Hunter to wear wraparound camouflage. Other points of interest include the matt finish with, as yet, only the unit motif and national insignia applied (in gloss); plus, as can be seen, the fin flash was incorrectly applied with blue leading red…! *Chris Ayre collection*

… while on the other side, the fin flash had been applied correctly. The other tails belong to 216 Squadron T.7 XL609 and T.7A XL568. *Chris Ayre collection*

216 Squadron motif. *Chris Ayre collection*

Photographed on 17 May 1958, the white wingtips and red fin code (outlined in yellow) on this F.6 appear to be the only relatively clean features of an otherwise very grimy XE584 'W' from 263 Squadron. Despite the grime, it is possible to discern the Squadron's motif and bars which by this time had been revised over those applied to their Hunter F.2s eighteen months earlier. Then the red bars flanking the motif had been narrower and thinly outlined in blue, but in this later form they were a little deeper with a yellow outline. Two blue crosses appeared on each bar in both versions, while the motif, a red lion rampant, continued to face forward on both sides of the nose while carrying a blue cross between its paws. *Newark Air Museum*

In 1967, Hunter F.6s (and T.7s) were allocated to 4 Flying Training School's No.3 Squadron to supplement, the School's diminutive Gnat T.1 trainers. At that time their F.6 fleet continued to appear much as they had when employed operationally, albeit a white disc with black code number now appeared on the nose, often repeated, initially at least, on the fin in a small-diameter disc. During this period some F.6s also wore the full 4 FTS badge in a standard frame on the fin as seen here on XG190 '70' in 1967, shortly before it was sold to India on 13 September that year… *Tony Buttler collection*

… whereas XG185 wears neither badge nor motif, but, apart from being commendably clean, it does display an unusual triangular-shaped device ahead of the '74' on its nose. *Tony Buttler collection*

Following on from the previous view of XG185, this later image shows the 4 FTS motif, a palm tree and pyramid, near the top of the fin. The 'diamond' immediately above the red segment of fin flash corresponds with the position of a small access panel. *Fred Martin collection*

When photographed in July 1973, 4 FTS XG185 '74', looked resplendent in the recently introduced high-visibility training aircraft colour scheme – comprising gloss Signal Red (BS 381C 537) and White fuselage with Light Aircraft Grey inner, and Signal Red outer, wing surfaces. XG185 came to grief on 21 April 1976 over Maltreath Sands, Wales, after a wing caught fire and the pilot ejected.

This image amply demonstrates the three principal colours used to create the high-visibility colour scheme introduced for training aircraft. Pristine 4 FTS F.6, XG164, seen at Chivenor in July 1975, lacked a code number, or at least one had yet to be applied.

A view of F.6, XF509 '73', selected to provide a glimpse of its under surfaces at Valley in July 1973.
*All: Fred Martin collection*

## A Note on ERUs

By this point it is likely that most readers will have noticed the (often) blue-coloured 'bumps' appearing near the wingtips on several F.6s, something that will become increasingly evident in many of the following photos from the F.6 onwards. What were they? For those who already know all about the ERU please bear with us – for those who do not then Mark Gauntlett kindly provides an explanation:

"The ERU is an 'Ejector Release Unit'. It's a device with an electrically-fired cartridge which is used to assist in releasing stores from the pylons – aircraft fitted with ERUs often have red warning triangles on the pylons. Earlier aircraft used EMRUs (Electro-Mechanical Release Units) to release stores but these provided much less 'assistance', relying primarily on gravity. To ensure stores departed cleanly, the ERU was introduced 'to help things along' – the released store being pushed away from the pylon by a piston within the unit. The bulge on the top of the wing covered the breech of the ERU (the inboard one didn't need a bulge as the wing was thick enough to contain the complete unit).

As for an ERU fairing's colour, if you look at an FGA.9 for example, you'll normally see that the bulge was coloured blue as it resides within the blue ring of the roundel. Of course, exceptions occurred and in the case of T.7 WV383 its roundels were positioned differently whereby all three colours covered the bulge to provide a tricolour effect.

On a related note, the little fins on the back of 100-gallon drop tanks were added for the same purpose. During trials it was found that the tanks could bump into the wing when jettisoned, so fins were added to 'nose down' the tank when released to help separation and guide it away cleanly. The 230-gallon tanks were braced and stressed for combat manoeuvres and not normally jettisoned of course, so they had no fins".

F.6, XF453 'V', seen c September 1963, while operating with the Day Fighter Combat School wearing 63 Squadron's miniature black and yellow chequered bars with motif on its nose. Having disbanded as an operational unit on 30 October 1958, its number plate was resurrected as a reserve unit one month later and within a short period of time was in use with the DFCS. Whereas XF453 displays a white spine, fin and wing stripes, other photos exist showing it with a red spine etc., but whether white preceded red remains unknown to the authors. Following a period of storage XF453 was bought by HSA on 14 July 1967. *Newark Air Museum*

Many will recognize XF418 as the focus of a Revell 1/72 kit, a Corgi die-cast model and the subject of numerous illustrations as well, thus it became a source of much deliberation – do we include it or not? All things considered, readers can at least compare this view of F.6 XF418 with one taken at Brawdy in 1977 following its conversion to an F.6A (q.v.). This photo was taken at Waddington on 14 September 1963 when in use with the DFCS. 63 Squadron's motif and miniature bars are visible on the nose. *Author's collection*

Seen at Finningley in September 1963, DFCS F.6, XG204 'B', offers a further splash of colour, its white wingtips making the Hunter's extremities more visible on gun camera film. Later allocated to 4 FTS, XG204 descended at high speed and crashed into a stone wall killing its Lebanese pilot on 15 August 1969. No explanation for the crash was established. *Fred Martin collection*

229 OCU F.6, XF512 '34', seen at Coltishall in September 1969, is devoid of any unit badges or markings save for the code '34' on a weathered yellow disc on the fin. The aircraft in the background is Lightning T.4, XM970 '970' from 226 OCU, Middleton St George. *Fred Martin collection*

When the DFCS disbanded on 1 November 1965, the Weapon Instructor Flight was formed within 229 OCU which also acquired 63 Squadron's number plate. On 2 September 1974, 229 OCU effectively disbanded, its work taken on by the TWU which formed that day at Brawdy. On the same day, 63 Squadron, a reserve unit since 1958 officially became 63(Reserve) Squadron. Seen in July 1975, F.6, XE653 '28', exhibits 63(R) Squadron bars and motif, white wingtips and a white section of spine and fin. *Fred Martin collection*

F.6, XE656 '35', displays 63(R) Squadron markings at Chivenor in July 1975…

… a year on, in July 1976, and XE656 had been spruced up prior to its appearance at Greenham Common, the opportunity having been taken to make one or two detail changes in the interim. The 1976 Greenham Common Air Tattoo was the venue of a celebration commemorating the Hunter's 25th anniversary.

Taken at Chivenor in September 1972, this image shows 229 OCU F.6, XG152 '53', preparing for a sortie. Note that only the outer pylon carries the warning triangle associated with an ERU which, unusually carries a green drop tank bearing the letters 'SNEB'. The white fuselage bars with a single red arrowhead in each, represent 79 Squadron which emerged as a reserve squadron when 229 OCU, the parent unit, acquired 79's number plate on 2 January 1967. The nosewheel door is yellow with code '53' repeated in black. *All: Fred Martin collection*

Also at Chivenor in September 1972 was 229 OCU / 79 Squadron F.6, XG364 '34', with Red/White/Blue national markings and large diameter fin disc. *Fred Martin collection*

Long before its brief sojourn with 216 Squadron in July 1980, 229 OCU F.6, XF383, is seen at Alconbury on 17 June 1961 displaying 145 Squadron colours on its nose, the motif being a pale blue banner with '145' in red, while the two pennants were white with red crosses. Both the code '14' and serial were white. 145 was a reserve unit from October 1958 within 229 OCU, but whether 145 or 234 Squadron became the first reserve unit to identify itself as such by late 1958 is still debated. Ironically, they were never supposed to exist at all in peacetime as a directive had made clear, they were intended to exist only on paper until war itself *actually* threatened. As directives go, it didn't last long! In 1956, nominated reserve units were referred to as 'shadow squadrons', a label officially discarded when, within about a year, it was replaced by the term 'reserve squadrons'. *Newark Air Museum*

Seen at Chivenor in September 1972 is 229 OCU F.6, XF420 '29', exhibits 234 Squadron's black dragon on a white disc flanked by yellow-outlined black bars, each with eight red diamonds. Having disbanded as an operational unit on 15 July 1957, 234 Squadron's number plate was allocated to 229 OCU on 22 October 1958, the same date as 145 Squadron's number plate. *Fred Martin collection*

Seen in July 1975, unidentified F.6, '36', displays 234 Squadron's black dragon which, curiously, seems to be trotting along on all fours! On 2 September 1974 the unit had officially become 234(Reserve) Squadron, the same day that 229 OCU was replaced by the newly-created TWU. *Fred Martin collection*

Seen c1966/67, F.6, XF375 '6', was received by the Empire Test Pilots School in April 1963. Previously retained for trial purposes by the manufacturers (Armstrong Whitworth Aircraft) and then by English Electric at Warton, it is conceivable that some of the trials were in connection with tail parachutes – note the modified tail cone. At this time XF375 was painted overall Signal Red (BS 381C 537) with White fuselage decking, spine and fin. Adding to the effect, but hard to see, is a black tapering cheatline extending from the black nose cap, behind the ETPS badge, then further aft to the wing leading edge. *Tony Buttler collection*

Seen at Greenham Common in July 1976, still operated by the ETPS, XF375 had been repainted overall Light Aircraft Grey with Signal Red spine, fin, wingtips and underwing tanks after the ETPS relocated to Boscombe Down from Farnborough in 1968. The ETPS badge ahead of the ejection seat warning triangle has either been removed or become so faded as to be illegible! XF375 became 8736M at Cranwell in January 1982. *Fred Martin collection*

An undated photo of XE587, although the toned-down fin flash and matt camouflage on the replacement fin both suggest a post-1970 image. Seen wearing Light Aircraft Grey with Signal Red spine, wingtips and underwing tanks, XE587 was operated by various agencies throughout its life for test purposes, including trials towing a 30ft x 6ft target banner from a belly hook and the development of tail parachutes, a clue to which is its modified tail cone with distinctive 'lip'. Built as an F.6, XE587 underwent modifications that took it towards F.6A/FGA.9 standard, albeit without being redesignated. Conveniently though, XE587 also serves to take us neatly to the Hunter F.6A. *Tony Buttler collection*

# Hunter F.6A

By now an F.6A, XF418 is seen in 1977 when operating with the TWU at Brawdy. The use of high-viz colour schemes probably had less to do with being used by instructors to 'jump' TWU students, than it did with concerns raised over increased collision risks at low level. It is likely that further stimulus was added on 4 April 1977, when Buccaneer S.2B XW525, from 208 Squadron, encountered two Hunters at low level causing the Buccaneer to pull up violently to avoid a collision and in so doing shed part of its tailplane and crashed into Claerwen Reservoir in mid-Wales. Although it should not be said that Brawdy's vividly painted Hunters were never used to jump students, one wonders if the term 'jump' was a convenient carryover from CFE/DFCS days – an assumption made in the absence of more recent information? *Fred Martin collection*

**A Cautionary Tale**

The emergence of the F.6A, 'Interim' FGA.9 and the FGA.9, existing as they did alongside remaining F.6s, has sown confusion and disagreement over the years. Despite their long service lives, the many mods applied across the fleet, not to mention those applied to individual airframes too numerous to count, it is possible to illuminate *some* of the differences that separated an F.6A from an 'Interim' FGA.9 and the full-spec FGA.9: Mark Gauntlett explains:

*Several F.6 airframes were converted to F.6A standard, enhancing their ability to undertake ground attack operations. The main differences were the ability to carry 230-gallon tanks on the inboard pylons, the addition of a brake parachute, inclusion of an additional oxygen bottle (by removing the de-icing tank and associated equipment in the nose) and the deletion of the gun blast deflectors (deemed unnecessary at ground attack altitudes). A source of confusion for some arose when other F.6 conversions had emerged as 'Interim' FGA.9s. In fact, the two 'new' variants were very similar, the differences between them being confined to some minor avionic disparities and a slightly revised cockpit layout. Effectively, both the F.6A and 'Interim' FGA.9 almost matched the full FGA.9 specification except that both retained the F.6's original Avon 203 engine, whereas full-spec FGA.9s received the Avon 207.*

*The FGA.9 also featured several modifications which had begun to be introduced late in the F.6s service life. For example, Mod. 968 replaced the twin VHF radio installation with a single UHF system with standby facility; Mod. 378 introduced the Ferranti Mk.8 gyro gunsight (replacing the Mk.5) on a fixed rather than retractable mount and Mod. 1343 upgraded the IFF system to incorporate the civil SSR (Secondary Surveillance Radar) function allowing military Hunters to operate in civil airspace more easily. As a result of this modification, the small triangular-shaped IFF aerial, previously located on an off-centre mount on the spine of the F.6/F.6A, was relocated to a position approximately halfway between the cockpit windscreen and the nose cone. Typically, where Hunters are concerned, this can't be considered a completely foolproof recognition feature however, as modifications were often introduced separately from Mark changes (as mentioned above, a small number of late F.6s also featured this IFF upgrade and nose-mounted aerial).*

*As you will have noticed, the F.6A, Interim FGA.9 and FGA.9 all featured reprofiled tail cones with a distinctive 'upper lip' containing a braking parachute introduced due to the increased weight of those marks and to enhance their ability to operate in more tropical climates.*

**Opposite page, bottom:** TWU F.6A, XG172 '23', seen at Chivenor in July 1975 with white wings outboard of the inner pylon and white fin. Might this have been part of a high-viz experiment too?
*Fred Martin collection*

**This page, top:** F.6A, XJ634 '29', from 1TWU, seen at Finningley in September 1978. (The TWU became 1TWU when 2 TWU formed on 31 July 1978.) The badge displayed below XJ634's cockpit is that of the TWU; it being identical to the 229 OCU badge save for the wording which was amended to read 'TACTICAL WEAPONS UNIT'. The original 229 OCU legend 'DISCENDO DUCES' was also retained.
*Fred Martin collection*

**Upper:** F.6A, XG160 '22', 63(R) Squadron is seen at Brawdy in July 1984, when most remaining RAF single-seat Hunters were entering their final weeks of Service flying, although this airframe would continue to serve as 8831M at Scampton from 2 September 1984. A component of 1TWU, XG160 displays the TWU badge on its nose. By October 1978 the Squadron's chequered bars had been moved to the rear fuselage either side of the roundel.
*Fred Martin collection*

**Lower and bottom:** The two sides of 1TWU F.6A, XE606 '11', as seen in August 1981 wearing 79(R) Squadron bars either side of the fuselage roundel and the TWU badge on its nose. The Squadron had officially become 79(Reserve) Squadron on 2 September 1974.
*Fred Martin collection*

TWU F.6A, XF382 '15', 234(R) Squadron, seen at Greenham Common in July 1976. Note that the fin flash slightly overlaps the yellow disc – not an uncommon feature. Later operated by 79(R) Squadron, XF382 was withdrawn from use in July 1984, its camera having been earlier removed.

Seen at Finningley in September 1989 in a Light Aircraft Grey and Signal Red scheme, this much photographed Hunter, based at Boscombe Down for decades, was used by both the A&AEE and ETPS. Eventually, in 1999, XE601 became the last *single-seat* Hunter to fly in British military service. Built as an F.6 it was later converted to F.6A standard and subsequently brought up to the FGA.9 specification. Most sources agree that it was never formally reclassified – but given its braced 230-gallon tanks and reprofiled tail cone XE601 reposes here – as an F.6A.

Also taken at Finningley, this time in September 1994, XE601 had by now been repainted in the RAE's so-called 'Raspberry Ripple' scheme, with a thin white line separating the Signal Red cheatline from the Oxford Blue (BS 381C 105) lower fuselage. Here, XE601 carries smoke generators on each inboard pylon used to simulate chemical or biological attacks for troop training purposes.

F.6/F.6A hybrid, XG210, seen at Brawdy in March 1984 while on a flying visit from RAE Bedford. Finished in Signal Red, White and Oxford Blue, the latter colour almost obscures the fact that XG210 is fitted with a Hunter FR.10-type nose. *All: Fred Martin collection*

# Hunter FGA.9

Finally relieved of its day fighter role in 1963, the Hunter F.6 was already being reduced in numbers as early as 1958 as the RAF continued to be 'downsized' to suit the Exchequer's purse. However, a new requirement to procure a ground attack aircraft capable of replacing ageing Venoms resulted in 128 Hunter F.6s being scheduled in 1959 for an upgrade to FGA.9 standard; thirty-six of which emerged as the 'Interim' FGA.9. Most, if not all, were later upgraded to the full FGA.9 specification.

The FGA.9's capabilities more than confirmed its suitability as a replacement for the Venoms in the Middle and Far East; indeed, in 28 Squadron's case the FGA.9 also provided Hong Kong with the colony's sole air defence. At home, both 1 and 54 Squadron re-equipped with FGA.9s as a component of 38 Group's rapid-reaction force in 1960 which also included the Javelin FAW.7/FAW.9, Beverley C.1, Hastings C.2, Pioneer CC.1, Twin Pioneer CC.1, Belvedere HC.1, Sycamore HR.14 and Whirlwind HAR.2/HAR.10. Eventually replaced operationally by more modern types, the FGA.9 would be extensively used in second-line roles for years afterwards.

**Above:** Unidentified FGA.9 'D' from 1 Squadron – date unknown. Having re-equipped with the FGA.9, UK-based 1 and 54 Squadron formed the ground attack element of 38 Group (reformed 1 January 1960) for operations both at home and abroad as required. *Author's collection*

**Below left:** 1 Squadron motif on an unidentified FGA.9 at Khormaksar, Aden. Both 1 and 54 Squadrons operated with the Aden Strike Wing when required. The latter has also been referred to variously as the Khormaksar Hunter Wing and Khormaksar Tactical Wing. Because none of these names seem ever to have been officially promulgated we sided with Aden Strike Wing! *Fred Martin collection*

**Below:** Carrying in total sixteen 60lb rockets, 8 Squadron FGA.9, XG256 'H', is seen operating over the inhospitable and mountainous surroundings of the Radfan, an area located near the border of Aden and Yemen, which became the scene of several British military actions against rebel tribesmen during the Radfan uprising in 1964. The uprising was one of many actions fought during the Aden Emergency which began in October 1963 and lasted until British forces were finally withdrawn from Aden in November 1967. Needless to say, FGA.9s featured prominently in the support of British ground forces. The harsh environment was harsh on aircraft too! *Tony Buttler collection*

FGA.9, XJ692 'T', seen here wearing joint unit markings combining 8 Squadron (left) with 43 Squadron (right) at Khormaksar during the Emergency. *Fred Martin collection*

A further example of joint unit markings as seen on FGA.9, XF376 'Q' with 8 Squadron bars on the fuselage and 208 Squadron's arrowhead with motif on the nose, while XE609 'E', behind, displays 208 marks only as does the one beyond that. The colour variations in respect of codes, serial numbers and nosewheel doors speak for themselves. 208 Squadron departed for Sharjah, UAE, in June 1964. The two towering transports are: left, a Beverley C.1; right, a 70 Squadron Hastings C.2. *Fred Martin collection*

FGA.9, XJ683 'F', which joined 20 Squadron at Tengah on 15 May 1964. The Squadron motif features a black eagle perched on a sword in front of a rising sun, all on a white disc. The bars either side of the motif are pale blue with three equal width horizontal stripes coloured, from the top, red, white and green. The fin code is white, thinly outlined in black and was repeated on the nosewheel door in black. XJ683 carries six, not eight, RPs under each outer wing section. Each outer wing section was subdivided into four stations, identified as A to D (outboard to inboard) and in order to carry RPs **on all four** stations the pylon at station B would need to be removed **or** have an adaptor rail fitted to the pylon. Either way, the RPs at Station B sat a little further aft than the others due to the pylon's location. Here, the tip of the pylon is visible and is not fitted with an adapter, hence six missiles per wing at stations A, C and D. *Newark Air Museum*

20 Squadron FGA.9, XK138 'M', seen in 1966, looking particularly careworn.
*Tony Buttler collection*

FGA.9, XE622 'A', 28 Squadron. Having operated the Venom FB.4 since November 1959, 28 Squadron re-equipped with the Hunter FGA.9 from May 1962, retaining them until the unit disbanded on 2 January 1967. During that time, 28 Squadron provided Hong Kong with its sole ground attack capability as well as a fig leaf air defence. The Squadron motif, Pegasus over a fasces axe, is displayed on a white disc flanked by yellow-bordered dark blue bars: the white fin code was repeated on the nosewheel door in black. XE622's wing-tips are either white or perhaps yellow, both were used at times, although photos do exist elsewhere in which coloured tips are not evident. XE622 was damaged beyond repair at Kai Tak on 12 July 1966 following an engine explosion while starting.
*Tony Buttler collection*

When 43 Squadron re-equipped with the FGA.9 the markings they applied were identical to those used on their F.6s – and not so different from those seen on their F.4s either. The chequered fuselage bars, seen here on XF445 'R' suggest this is an early 1960s image as, by 1963, when the unit was based at Khormaksar, the bars had been relocated to the nose, either side of the unit's fighting cock (gamecock) motif. Of less interest perhaps, the strut normally associated with the 230-gallon tank is missing and gun blast deflectors are still fitted. Refurbished, XF445 was transferred to Chile in January 1983, a few months after the conclusion of the Falklands War.
*Tony Buttler collection*

FGA.9, XG169 'K', 43 Squadron, seen at Khormaksar on an unknown date, but probably 1965 or later given that the checks have migrated back to the rear fuselage (see previous caption) while the wingtips are plain white (i.e. non-chequered).
*Fred Martin collection*

A 1973 photo of 45 Squadron FGA.9, XG264 'J'. The Squadron had reformed at West Raynham with FGA.9s prior to moving to Wittering in September 1972 tasked with the operational training of pilots for the new Jaguar ground attack aircraft.
*Tony Buttler collection*

45 Squadron FGA.9, XK138 '67', Wittering, May 1975. The yellow tag on the ladder states 'ARMED', and a wing commander's pennant is visible below the cockpit sill. The airman on the ground appears to be loading a sub-munition into the pod on the outer pylon. Allocated to 45 squadron in 1973, XK138 later served with the TWU, 2TWU then 1TWU prior to being transferred to Chile in May 1982.
*Fred Martin collection*

Pristine 45 Squadron FGA.9, XK137 '42', seen at Greenham Common in July 1976, the month 45 Squadron disbanded. Previously numbered '66', and reportedly coded 'D' prior to that, the board under the nose reads "HAWKER SIDDELEY HUNTER FGA MK 9 EX 45 SQUADRON RAF BRAWDY". Thus, when photographed, it was already carrying its TWU number '42'. Doubtless the unit markings seen here were soon removed, but for the moment they were retained in readiness for the Hunter's 25th anniversary celebration held at Greenham Common. This photo shows the 45 Squadron colours and motif to near perfection, only the pale blue outline around the white disc, and the black fuselage serial numbers need pointing out. Following the earlier demise of 58 Squadron, both 45 Squadron and the parent Wittering Hunter Wing were disbanded on 26 July 1976. *Fred Martin collection*

FGA.9, XF523 'N', from 54 Squadron, seen c1963, was operated by this unit both prior to and following its modification to FGA.9 standard. As stated, both 1 and 54 Squadrons had their roles recast to provide tactical air support for 38 Group, Transport Command. Epitomized for ground attack duties the FGA.9's primary weapon was the 3in rocket projectile of which a maximum of sixteen could be carried in two tiers. The 3in RPs were later replaced by MATRA rocket pods. *Tony Buttler collection*

Taken from the same sequence as the previous photo, this aspect of XF523 'N' provides additional detail. XF523 was destroyed when it crashed on 24 June 1963 at Benina, Airport, Libya, following a series of unauthorized low-level aerobatics: the pilot was killed. *Tony Buttler collection*

Nose detail of an unidentified 54 Squadron FGA.9 at Khormaksar. *Fred Martin collection*

Unidentified 54 Squadron FGA.9 seen at Khormaksar, by which point the yellow disc on the fin had been discarded and the fin code returned to yellow. *Fred Martin collection*

FGA.9, XF519 '90', from 58 Squadron, seen at Wittering on an unknown date. Reformed on 1 August 1973 to provide a pool of highly trained ground attack pilots alongside 45 Squadron, 58 Squadron was disbanded on 4 June 1976, its role being taken on by the TWU. The white disc containing the unit's owl motif perched on a branch is thinly outlined in pale blue, as are the two bars. *Fred Martin collection*

FGA.9, XG252 '87', from 58 Squadron seen at Leuchars. *Fred Martin collection*

FGA.9, XE532 'K', from 208 Squadron, is seen at Khormaksar where the unit had arrived in November 1961 to join the Aden Strike Wing. Converted to FGA.9 standard in 1964, it was coded 'K' on joining 208 and then 'A' in November 1964. Typically the unit's Hunters wore white wingtips, in which case XE532 is somewhat untypical. This aircraft was lost on 6 May 1968 when it struck a radio mast and lost power, forcing the pilot to (safely) eject over the sea near Dubai. *Tony Buttler collection*

FGA.9, XK140 'D', from 208 Squadron. Having previously served twice with this unit coded 'E' and 'H' respectively, XK140 returned to 208 for a five-week period commencing 26 April 1967 – this time as 'D'. Returned to the UK, it served with several units, the last being 2TWU which operated XK140 until 3 July 1979, the day on which the pilot lost control and ejected during a low-level exercise north of Ullapool. *Fred Martin collection*

Unidentified 208 Squadron FGA.9 seen at Khormaksar. The unit's arrowhead and Gizah (Giza) sphinx motif are seen alongside 8 Squadron's badge. *Fred Martin collection*

1TWU FGA.9, XG155 '1', seen at Finningley in September 1981. *Fred Martin collection*

Two 2TWU FGA.9s, XK138 'S' and XG261 'J', seen taking off from Binbrook in April 1980, about a month before the latter crashed near Dufftown, Grampian, following loss of control during air combat training on 28 May. (See also image of XK138 when serving with 45 Squadron.) *Fred Martin collection*

Notorious as the Hunter that flew under Tower Bridge in 1968, this image shows FGA.9, XF442 'V', in a less exacting pose in July 1975 while being operated by the TWU's 63(R) Squadron. XF442 was sold to Chile in April 1982 as part of Britain's agreement to supply Hunters, Canberras and other material useful to the Chilean government in return for mutually beneficial military support following Argentina's invasion of the Falkland Islands on 2 April that year. *Fred Martin collection*

**Top and above:** F.6A XE608 '12', seen at Coningsby in July 1981, offers a rare view of the Hunter's upper surfaces, while FGA.9, XG194 'A', displays its grimy underside to equally good effect.
*Both Fred Martin Collection*

**Left:** 1TWU / 234(R) Squadron FGA.9, XE624 'G', seen at Brawdy in June 1984. One wonders if the lessons of the fifties and sixties had been forgotten twenty or so years later, i.e., the staining caused by engine cooling exhausts to fuselage bars when placed in the 'low' position as opposed to 'high'!
*Fred Martin collection*

# Hunter FR.10

Following a trial installation of a five-camera reconnaissance nose on a Hunter F.4, the Ministry of Supply issued a requirement for a simpler three-camera nose to be fitted to Hunter F.6 airframes which by 1958 were being withdrawn from service in increasing numbers. F.6, XF429, became the prototype FR.10 and first flew in its new guise on 7 November 1959. Thirty-two further conversions followed. Essentially, excluding mods specific to the FR.10, all thirty-three received the same basic modifications as the FGA.9, including the replacement of the Avon 203 engine with the Avon 207.

A front-aspect view of prototype Hunter FR.10, XF429, taken in 1959 but prior to its first flight in its new guise. *Tony Buttler collection*

A 2 Squadron Swift FR.5 accompanied by three of its replacements, the Hunter FR.10, c February 1961. *Newark Air Museum*

FR.10, XJ633 'S', served with 2 Squadron from 29 January 1970 until 2 March 1971, following which it departed the unit and went to HSA. Compared to the previous image it can be seen that small changes of style were applied to the unit's markings during the 1960s whereby the fuselage bars were moved to the 'high' position to avoid damage, and the code letter on the fin changed from white to black, now on a white triangle. 2 Squadron's fuselage bars were narrower than those used by 4 Squadron, with which XJ633 had previously served; their removal accounting for the merest ghost of discolouration (visible on the original photo) that rises to a point level with the top of the roundel. Squadron Leader R.J.M. David's pennant can be seen above the gun port. *Fred Martin collection*

This 4 Squadron FR.10, XF428 'C', has been 'zapped', probably during a joint fighter-reconnaissance exercise. A German iron cross, plus 'Snoopy' in an RF-84 Thunderflash (at least that's what it looks like) are evident ahead of the wing root but, most elaborate of all, a 306 Squadron Royal Netherlands Air Force badge dominates the fin. Both the RNLAF and the Luftwaffe operated the RF-84. *Tony Buttler collection*

XF428 served with 4 Squadron from 25 January 1961 to July 1965 prior to going to 2 Squadron where it remained until sold to HSA in July 1971. These two views of XF428 illustrate the relative positions of the FR.10's camera ports on either side of the nose – the port camera faced directly to the side to 'shoot' parallel to the Hunter's line of flight, whereas the starboard camera was angled slightly downwards.

FR.10, XE614 'RJ', from 1417 Flight, Khormaksar, displaying the Flight's arrowhead marking and motif on the nose. The message 'NO HYDRAULICS' is chalked beneath the cockpit, below which sits an unintelligible message on a white card. 1417 Flight reformed out of 8 Squadron's reconnaissance element at Khormaksar on 1 March 1963 to operate with 8, 43 and 208 Squadrons as part of the Aden Strike Wing. Having obtained four FR.10s from 8 Squadron, it also acquired four T.7s from the Khormaksar Station Flight. 1417 Flight was reabsorbed by 8 Squadron on 8 June 1967. *Both: Fred Martin collection*

**Right:** FR.10, XF460 'DB', from 1417 Flight with an Andover beyond. Apparently, the Flight's two-letter code system reflected the initials of a given pilot, this Hunter having at various times also been coded 'GT', 'KS' and 'RB'. Of related interest, it is known that the nosewheel door of Flt Lt R Pyrah's FR.10 was painted powder blue with his initials 'RP' applied in red. *Fred Martin collection*

**Below left:** 1417 Flight's 'arrowhead' containing RAF Station Khormaksar's badge. *Fred Martin collection*

**Below:** Having been phased out of operational service, several FR.10s obtained a further lease of life with 229 OCU. Here, white-spined XF426 '12', from 229 OCU undergoes maintenance at Finningley eighteen months prior to being sold to the Royal Jordanian Air Force in March 1972. *Fred Martin collection*

**Bottom:** 229 OCU FR.10, XG168 '10', displays its 79 Squadron markings *c*1971. Seen earlier as F.6 'G-W' of 208 Squadron, this Hunter was sold to Jordan on 22 March 1972, about two and a half years before 79 became 79(R) Squadron. *Tony Buttler collection*

# Two-seat Hunters

Perceived initially as unnecessary, the RAF did eventually order small quantities of two-seat Hunters which, forward-looking as ever, had already been developed as a private venture by Hawkers with a view to overseas sales in mind. Their two-seat prototype, XJ615, had first flown on 8 July 1955 and it was around this airframe that an RAF specification was written resulting in small numbers of new-build T.7s being procured, supplemented by a smaller number of conversions using redundant F.4 airframes.

In total the RAF received forty-five new T.7s plus six converted F.4s, but as the appendices (q.v.) reveal, ten further new-build T.7s were diverted to the Fleet Air Arm to become the T.8. (The FAA also acquired 31 conversions from ex-F.4 stocks which became T.8, T.8B and T.8C as appropriate).

While the information provided explains the number of two-seaters procured, the reader is advised to keep in mind the bewildering array of T.7/T.8 transfers that were to occur in the decades following the type's introduction to service involving RAF, RAE and FAA stocks alike. It is also useful to recall that while the airfield arrester hook fitted to the T.8 ought to distinguish it from a T.7, both had interchangeable rear fuselage sections which would later render some T.8s 'hookless' while some T.7s became 'hookers'. To add further diversity, a small number of two-seaters later received upgrades specific to themselves, leading to further designations being introduced such as the T.7A and T.8M.

In retrospect, we can marvel at how useful this 'unnecessary' two-seater became

– it outlived all the single seat Hunters in British service!

To avoid unnecessary duplication, where a unit's colours/markings have already received mention they will not be repeated again in this section.

## 12, 15, 16, 208, 216 Sqns and 237 OCU

In February 1980, Buccaneer XV345 crashed during an exercise at Nellis Air Force Base in the USA, consequently the entire Buccaneer fleet was grounded while fatigue checks were conducted. During the following months the Buccaneer squadrons became 'all-Hunter' units as several additional Hunters were drafted in to augment the existing 'twin-stick' Hunter fleet. After a period of six months or so, the Buccaneers began to filter back into service once the inspection programmes and necessary remedial work had been completed.

*See Appendix 2 for details of RAF training units and Appendix 3 for RN units.*

Hawker P.1101, XJ615, the Hunter T.7 prototype. Conceived by the manufacturer who had foreseen the need for a two-seat Hunter, this F.4-based airframe retained 'straight' wing leading edges while all subsequent T.7/T.8 derivatives were completed with leading-edge wing extensions. Despite RAF hopes that their 'twin-stickers' would be based on the F.6 with its powerful 'big-bore' engine, all (except for the T.12) retained 'small-bore' Avons. Operated by the ETPS, XJ615 crashed into high ground near Hazelmere, Surrey, on 24 June 1964 killing the *Armée de l'Air* pilot. *Tony Buttler collection*

Hunter T.7, WV372 'R', from 2 Squadron as seen at Gütersloh in July 1970. By March 1971 it was serving with the RAE before later going to 4 FTS. Ultimately sold in February 1997, tragically, WV372 would crash at Shoreham on 22 August 2015. *Fred Martin collection*

Hunter T.7, XL621 'L', from 4 Squadron also seen at Gütersloh in 1970. *Fred Martin collection*

T.7, XF321 'TZ', was one of the six F.4s converted to T.7 standard for the RAF, following which it was used by 43 and 8 Squadrons whose colours are seen left and right of the roundel respectively. In August 1965, XF321 was allocated to 1417 Flight whose arrowhead appears on the nose, albeit the white disc is empty. Having later served with the FAA, XF321 was returned and later allocated to the RAE who operated it until it was written-off in July 1984 following an unintended wheels-up landing. *Fred Martin collection*

12 Squadron reformed as a Buccaneer S.2 unit in October 1969 and was never a Hunter unit *per se*, but because a dedicated Buccaneer trainer was never procured, several two-seat Hunters were used to assist in familiarizing aircrew with the Buccaneer. Here T.7, XL573 is seen, in July 1987, wearing a wraparound camouflage scheme with 12 Squadron's fox-head motif with a Roman XII between its ears. The pale blue fin code '573' was a recent change – it had been 'WC'. *Fred Martin collection*

Three years later, now with reduced-size national markings and a repainted wraparound camouflage scheme, XL573 is seen in 1990 during its final few months of active service. XL573 went to Shawbury for storage in March 1991 and was sold in December 1993. *Newark Air Museum*

15 Squadron, also a Buccaneer S.2 unit was, along with 16 Squadron, based in West Germany. Seen at Brüggen rather than its home base Laarbruch in July 1972 is T.7A, WV318, with only the Squadron number adorning the fin, while the nosewheel door simply carried the code '318', the 'last three' of the serial, in black. Built as an F.4, WV318 was converted to a T.7 in 1959, then further upgraded to T.7A standard in late 1964. To some it will always be a T.7B, although it doesn't appear to have been officially recognised as such.

T.7A, WV318, as seen ten years later with obvious changes in appearance requiring no further elaboration except perhaps to mention the acquisition of an airfield arrester hook. Ostensibly still serving with 15 Squadron, 1982 was the year in which all Laarbruch's Hunters were taken over by the Station Flight, a clue to which was the appearance (in some instances) of a small penguin motif on the aircraft's nose, as seen here above the nosewheel door. Both: *Fred Martin collection*

T.7, XL600, was first issued to 65 Squadron in early 1959, then later to 111 Squadron before gravitating to 4 FTS in 1967 where it remained until 1980 (the last 4 FTS Hunters having eventually been replaced by Hawks late in 1979 or early 1980). Transferred to 16 Squadron, XL600 is seen here in May 1981 with 4 FTS colours and markings still evident, the only apparent change appears to be the substitution of the 4 FTS motif with 16 Squadron's black and yellow 'Saint' motif. XL600 was transferred to RNAY Fleetlands on 17 October 1984 and became maintenance airframe A2729: it was placed on the disposal list on 30 August 1991. *Fred Martin collection*

**Right:** Uncoded 19 Squadron T.7, XL594, with Squadron badge and bars on the nose, as seen at Leconfield in late 1960 complete with yellow training bands ('T-bands'). Later coded 'K', XL594 was destroyed on 16 April 1964 when it struck rising ground while practising aerobatics.
*Fred Martin collection*

**Above:** Hooked 45 Squadron T.7, XL619, seen at Wittering in August 1975 with what appears to be a replacement fin. It's possible that the new section has been coated with a primer that looks very similar to the green primer often used at the time to which a pale blue '77' was temporarily applied. Later photos show it with a white code correctly positioned on the fin i.e., larger and moved further aft toward the rudder. The code was repeated in black, on the nosewheel door. XL619 crashed on 21 October 1981 after being abandoned during an inverted spin.
*Fred Martin collection*

**Above left:** Following on from the earlier photo of T.7, XL600 – albeit not chronologically, this image was taken c1960 when serving with 65 Squadron.
*Newark Air Museum*

**Left:** One of two T.7s used by 74 Squadron, XL620 'Z', is seen in August 1963 with yellow T-bands. XL620 was unusual (but not unique) in that having been sold to HSA and then delivered to Saudi Arabia on 2 May 1966, it was later returned to Britain to re-enter service as XX466. Thereafter it was used variously by the RAF, RAE and RN/FRADU, latterly as A2738 (from May 1986), until finally being withdrawn from use on 22 March 1993. *Author's collection*

74 Squadron's other T.7 was XL568 'X', seen here at Coltishall on 13 August 1963. It is included because this seems to have been the period when yellow T-bands were generally being replaced by fluorescent paints or day-glo, although it doesn't appear to have 'weathered' particularly well! Coltishall-based 74 Squadron re-equipped with the Lightning F.1 in June 1960, but in common with many RAF squadrons at this time Hunter T.7s were still in evidence. XL568 was converted to T.7A standard in 1963 and remained active until finally retired from flying duties (with 208 Squadron) in late 1993 or early 1994, after which it became 9224M at Cranwell. *Author's collection*

92 Squadron T.7, XL605 'T' seen between August 1959, when the Squadron's new style motif (a cobra head with single maple leaf) was introduced, but before it became a 'Blue Diamond' in 1961. Sold to Saudi Arabia on 7 June 1966, XL605 was later passed to Jordan before it was returned to Britain and the RAF in May 1972 – now serialled XX467. Following service with 229 OCU and the TWU it was SOC in October 1983 and became a ground instruction airframe. At the time of writing (July 2018) XL605/XX467 resides at the Newark Air Museum. *Tony Buttler collection*

Still carrying 'Blue Diamond' colours, 92 Squadron T.7, XL605 'T', is seen at Leconfield. As stated earlier, the Squadron formed the RAF's official aerobatic team for the 1961-1962 season. However, this must be a later image given that the unit re-equipped with the Lightning F.2 in March 1963, as proven by the two blue fins looming over XL605 which display the unit's resurrected, earlier-style motif with full-length cobra and two maple leaves. Not visible here was another amendment, 92 Squadron replaced the chequered markings previously carried by their Hunters with an arrowhead device containing red and yellow chevrons on the nose of their Lightnings (until 1968 that is!) *Fred Martin collection*

Built as an F.4 and later converted to T.8 standard, XE665 was delivered as such to the FAA in 1959. In storage by August 1979, XE665 was loaned to the RAF from April 1980 to April 1984 to help alleviate a shortage of two-seat Hunters for use by RAF Buccaneer units. Having returned to service with FRADU, XE665 remained in use until placed in storage at Shawbury in April 1995, four months prior to being sold. Still looking much as it did in FAA service, finished in overall Light Aircraft Grey with day-glo (or Signal Red paint!) nose, fin and wing panels, XE665 is seen at Abingdon in 1982: only the 208 Squadron motif on the nose and their 'winged-eye' motif on the fin serve to confirm that it was (temporarily) in the hands of a new custodian. *Fred Martin collection*

208 Squadron T.7, XL591, in the Dark Green/Dark Sea Grey upper surfaces and Light Aircraft Grey undersides scheme with low-vis Red/Blue national markings, 208 Squadron motif on the nose and the 'winged-eye' on the fin, seen in June 1982 at Honington. *Fred Martin collection*

Last seen operating with 15 Squadron in 1972 and Laarbruch's Station Flight in 1982, this photo catches up with T.7A, WV318, four years later in September 1986 while serving as 'M' with 208 Squadron. Although seen at Marham, 208 had been based at Lossiemouth since 1983. *Fred Martin collection*

Photographed at Boscombe Down on 10 June 1990, T.7, XL591 '591', was still active with 208 Squadron although by this time its appearance had altered considerably compared to eight years earlier, courtesy of the small-diameter Red/Blue national markings, wraparound camouflage, and a truly minute 208 Squadron motif behind the cockpit. XL591 served until March 1991. Later stored at Shawbury, it was sold in early 1994. *Author's collection*

Late of 4 FTS and 237 OCU, T.7 XL609, was allocated to 216 Squadron after the latter re-formed on 1 July 1979. Intended to become the third UK-based Buccaneer squadron (plus OCU), the unit was never able to fully establish itself because of the fatigue issues which would soon become apparent; consequently 216 was absorbed by 12 Squadron on 4 August 1980. The 216 Squadron motif, an eagle carrying a bomb is clearly visible, as too is the T.7s single Aden cannon. Seen here at Lossiemouth in 1980, XL609 became 8866M there in July 1985 and was eventually broken up in 1993. *Chris Ayre collection*

Hunter T.7, XL586 'RS-90', in overall High-Speed Silver with white wingtips, is seen in 1958 or 1959 shortly after being delivered new to 229 OCU. At this time 229 OCU often applied one of two unit codes, either 'ES' or 'RS' to their aircraft (often in white on camouflaged Hunters).
*Tony Buttler collection*

Seen at Coltishall in September 1969, 229 OCU T.7, XL583 '91', displays its overall Light Aircraft Grey scheme with day-glo stripes and wing bands which displaced the yellow T-bands of an earlier period. A standard bomb carrier is fitted to the outboard pylon with two 28 lb practice bombs attached. Of note is the 'tricolour' ERU – a result of the upper wing roundel's position over the outer pylon. Only operated by 229 OCU and the TWU, XL583 was abandoned in flight on 1 December 1981 following engine failure on the approach to Brawdy.
*Fred Martin collection*

Thirteen or fourteen years later and XL586 was still with 229 OCU and still coded '90'. Now finished in the Dark Green/Dark Sea Grey over Light Aircraft Grey scheme, albeit with very glossy nose and tail sections, and still with Red/White/Blue national markings, this photo was taken at Chivenor in September 1972.
*Fred Martin collection*

This image of 229 OCU / 234 Squadron Hunter T.7, XL577 '82', in overall HSS with day-glo strips and white wingtips is included to illustrate the possibility that the man with the stencil might have made an error inasmuch as 234 Squadron's black dragon has been applied facing aft. Usually the dragon was meant to face forward on the port side and aft on the starboard. The numerals on the fin have an unusual style too. *Tony Buttler collection*

**Top left:** 229 OCU / 234 Squadron Hunter T.7, XL592 '93', as seen at Finningley in September 1963 with their motif placed behind the cockpit rather than on the nose and a forward-facing dragon. XL592 went to Scampton as 8836M on 31 August 1984 and was sold in May 1996. *Fred Martin collection*

**Top right:** As mentioned, 237 OCU was a Buccaneer unit to which various Hunters were allocated over the years in lieu of a dedicated Buccaneer trainer. XF967 was an ex-RN T.8C that was struck off RN charge on 13 November 1969 and immediately transferred to the RAF. Seen at Greenham Common in July 1976, XF967 displays 237 OCU's motif consisting of crossed cutlasses with black mortar superimposed and the code '967' on the nosewheel door. *Fred Martin collection*

**Above** Ex-4 FTS T.7, XL601, seen at Wattisham in August 1981 while serving with 237 OCU. The tiny diamond-shaped device on the nosewheel door contains the approximate silhouette of a Buccaneer with the Roman numeral 'XV' immediately below. As far as we can ascertain XL601 didn't serve with 15 Squadron, so is it a small-scale zap?

**Right:** Ex-F.4, ex-RN T.8, WV322, seen here at Mildenhall in July 1984, was transferred back to the RAF in May 1972 and allocated to 237 OCU with which it remained until it was assigned to Cranwell as 9096M *c*1997.

**Bottom:** Adding to the two earlier photos taken when serving with 12 Squadron (q.v.) in 1987 and 1990, this image of XL573 turns the clock backwards a little to May 1985 when, as 'WC', it was serving with 237 OCU. From 1981 onwards, XL573 rotated almost exclusively between these two units.
*All: Fred Martin collection*

Ten years on and T.8C, XF967, now coded 'V', had long since lost its glossy camouflage and Red/White/Blue national markings, all replaced by matt camouflage and toned-down national markings with a reduced size 237 OCU motif on a red disc below the cockpit. Seen in September 1986, this T.8 was destined to serve the OCU until it disbanded on 1 October 1991. Thereafter, XF967 was transferred to the Buccaneer Training Flight (BTF) which formed within 208 Squadron to maintain a training programme. When the BTF disbanded in late 1992, XF967 moved to 208 Squadron until it too disbanded in March 1994, although some sources suggest that it had already become 9186M at Cranwell by that date. *Fred Martin collection*

T.7, XL613 '613' from 237 OCU, seen at Waddington in April 1988. Stored at Shawbury from March 1991, XL613 was sold in December 1993 or early in 1994.

T.7, XL565, from 237 OCU, seen at Finningley in September 1990 with reduced size national markings and even smaller motif situated just behind the cockpit. Stored at Shawbury from 22 March 1991, XL565 had been sold and removed by late January 1994. *Both: Fred Martin collection*

**Top, left and centre:** In 1991, Air Chief Marshal Sir Patrick Hine, GCB, GBE, retired from the RAF, and to honour him a few Hunters were painted overall matt black (not gloss) to commemorate his days as a pilot with the famous 'Black Arrows' of 111 Squadron in the late 1950s. Thus, T.7A WV318 'A' (seen here in July 1991): T.8C XF967 'B', (seen September 1992): T.7A XL568 'C' and T.7A XL616 'D' (pictured together in December 1992 with 'C' nearest), were the four airframes selected. Speculation that a fifth, XL614, was also painted black remains unproven to the author who has yet to find an image of an all-black XL614. As to which unit the all-black Hunters pictured here belonged to is problematical – it depends on the date that each photo was taken. In 1991, it seems likely that all four would have been grouped within 237 OCU for the event itself, however, on 1 October the OCU disbanded and the four airframes reallocated (assuming they hadn't been already). WV318 went to 12 Squadron it seems and the others to 208 Squadron and/or the related Buccaneer Training Flight. By late 1992, after the demise of the BTF, both 12 and 208 were pooling their resources until the former disbanded in October 1993, while 208 Squadron, the last RAF unit to fly the Hunter, disbanded on 31 March 1994.

**Bottom:** T.7, XL571 '99', from the TWU seen at Chivenor in July 1975. XL571 was abandoned over the St George's Channel on 8 September 1977 due to engine failure, both crewmen ejecting safely.
*All Fred Martin collection*

T.7, XL595 '78', from 1 TWU / 79(R) Squadron at Brawdy in July 1984. *Fred Martin collection*

Adding to the earlier photos of XL591 when it was serving with 208 Squadron, the T.7 is seen here many years earlier, in 1967, when it was with 4 FTS coded '82' and well before the eye-catching gloss Red, Light Aircraft Grey and White colour scheme of the 1970s was introduced. *Fred Martin collection*

On 1 January 1969 the Harrier Conversion Team was established at Wittering to convert operational pilots to the Harrier GR.1. On 1 April 1970, the unit's name was changed to the Harrier Conversion Unit which remained in force until the HCU became 233 OCU on 1 October 1970. Because Harrier T.2s had yet to enter service, small numbers of Hunters were attached for use by instructors as chase 'planes to accompany pilots converting to the Harrier GR.1. The use of Hunter FGA.9s in this role is reasonably well known, FGA.9, XF430 'N', for example, was one of the small number thus employed. However, two T.7s, XL596 '1' and XL601 '2' were also attached to the unit – the former being illustrated here during its brief two-month allocation to the unit from June 1970. Whereas XL601 remained long enough to become part of 233 OCU, XL596 went to 4 Squadron by then equipped with Harriers. It was destroyed in a fatal crash near Shawbury on 2 November 1973 while operating with 4 FTS. *Fred Martin collection*

Certain readers 'of a certain age' may recall airshows in the eighties where, occasionally, the opportunity arose to view instructional airframes 8676M '01' (T.7, née XL577), and 8685M '99' (F.6A, née XF516) in the 'static' wearing an unusual motif on a white disc and wondered what it represented – I know I (MD) did! Both Hunters (there were others too) were based at Cranwell and belonged to the Servicing Instructional Flight which maintained taxyable instructional airframes, several of which displayed a white disc on the nose. The disc, thinly outlined in red and flanked by two red bars divided by a horizontal white stripe, contained the SIS 'Teacher Owl' on a branch with a mortarboard upon its head and a cane under the left wing. *(SIS information courtesy of Mick Coombes c/o Newark Air Museum) Author's collection*

ETPS T.7, XL579 '25', from RAE Farnborough seen in September 1966 a couple of years before the unit relocated to Boscombe Down in 1968. Seen in the standard ETPS scheme of the day, XL579 was finished in (reportedly) overall Signal Red with a White fuselage spine and fin and black anti-glare panel. Part of a nose probe protrudes from the black nose 'cap'. The panel below the cockpit contains the ETPS badge, the whole edged by the words 'Empire Test Pilots School'. XL579 crashed on the approach to Boscombe Down on 22 January 1976. *Author's collection*

Unrecognisably different in appearance from its later matt all-black colour scheme, XL616 had been sold to the Ministry of Technology in December 1967 before returning to the RAF in 1980. Photographed in 1968 or 1969, XL616 was then serving with the ETPS at Boscombe Down painted in overall Light Aircraft Grey with Signal Red fuselage, cockpit, spine, empennage, wingtips and tanks. The ETPS badge sits behind the cockpit, while a black anti-glare panel (removed c1970) is located in front.

T.7, XL612 '2', from the ETPS, seen at Fairford in July 1994 with a replacement fin, but otherwise finished in the 'Raspberry Ripple' scheme consisting of Oxford Blue, Signal Red and White with black anti-glare panel. Resident with the ETPS for many years, XL612 was officially retired on 10 August 2001, the date that marked the last flight of the last operational Hawker Hunter flying with the UK military. *Both: Fred Martin collection*

XF289, '777/BY', belonging to Brawdy-based 738 NAS, seen in a well-worn overall HSS, with day-glo nose, fin and wing panels, and the unit's Pegasus motif on its nose. XF289 joined the Squadron on 1 April 1965, but from June 1966 it was in workshop hands for upgrading to T.8C standard prior to being returned to 738 five months later still marked '777/BY'. The photo is believed to date from mid-1965 when it was a T.8, but if it dates from late 1966 onwards then it's a T.8C. XF289 remained in service until sold in 1994.

In what appears to be another well-worn HSS with day-glo panels scheme, T.8C, XF991 '688/LM', of 764 NAS seen at Lossiemouth c1970 is fitted with a standard bomb carrier on the outer pylon. The unit markings – white scales on a black disc – are flanked by green and white checks. XF991 was destroyed when it crashed near Martock, Somerset, on 24 May 1978.

To assist pilots converting to the Sea Harrier FRS.1 and its nose-mounted Blue Fox radar, two Blue Fox-equipped Hunter T.8Ms, XL580 and XL603 were converted, re-finished in the Extra Dark Sea Grey and White scheme and then delivered to 899 NAS at Yeovilton. XL580 '717/VL', with winged fist motif on its fin, is seen here at Yeovilton in August 1982, twelve months after being delivered to the unit in T.8M form. It later acquired the code '719/VL' and later still '723'. XL580 last flew on 27 August 1993, and in 1994 went to the FAA Museum. (Note that T.8M prototype, XL602, wasn't issued to 899 NAS.)

The other T.8M allocated to 899 NAS was XL603 '720' seen here finished in Extra Dark Sea Grey over White at Yeovilton in March 1988, its reprofiled (radar) nose being more easily appreciated from this angle. Sidewinder acquisition rounds are fitted to the outer pylons: six years earlier the Sea Harrier and its Blue Fox/Sidewinder missile combination had proven lethal against Argentine air forces. *All: Fred Martin collection*

T.8M, XL603 once again. Having spent the period from November 1989 to February 1992 with Lovaux Ltd at Hurn, presumably for maintenance and modification, XL603 returned to 899 NAS coded '724' and repainted overall Dark Sea Grey with low-viz national markings. XL603 made its last flight, prior to being sold, on 25 June 1993. *Newark Air Museum*

Turning the clock back to July 1971, XL580 '743/VL', is again seen at Yeovilton albeit several years prior to its conversion to one of three T.8Ms. In 1971 it was being operated by Airwork Ltd.'s Air Direction Training Unit (ADTU) which provided aircraft for the Navy's Fighter Direction School. XL580 is finished in overall HSS with a black anti-glare panel and FAA-style day-glo panels with the unit's recently simplified double 'speedbird' motif on the nose (a stylised 'D' forms its 'eye'). Part of the aircraft's code is repeated on the nosewheel door. In December 1972, ADTU merged into FRADU. *Both: Fred Martin collection*

It is likely that these two images of WT722 date from the late 1970s or early 1980s and certainly before September 1982 when it was recoded '878/VL' and then retained until sold in July 1995. Other than the replacement fin section, WT722 is finished in the post-1969 T.8 overall Light Aircraft Grey scheme with day-glo orange panels. *Chris Ayre collection*

Fitted with a Harley light in its extreme nose (used for visual tracking), T.8C, WT722 '873', had clearly been returned to FRADU service following an overhaul that included a replacement ex-RAF camouflaged fin complete with fin flash. The Harley light was fitted in May 1972 when WT722 was in ADTU hands coded '742/VL', which changed to '872/VL' with FRADU, then changed again in February 1975 to '873/VL'. Presumably 'VL' would have been restored to the fin after it was repainted? *Chris Ayre collection*

FRADU T.8C, WV363 '872/VL', seen in December 1987 at Yeovilton finished in overall Dark Sea Grey (DSG) with low-viz national markings. WV363 came to grief on 13 December 1990 when it caught fire and had to be abandoned over the sea 70 miles north of the Isle of Lewis. *Fred Martin collection*

As with the RAF, the FAA also operated station flights, about sixty-four of them over the decades all told, but only a small handful survived long enough to receive a Hunter. One that did was the Hal Far Station Flight at Malta, and one of its Hunters, T.8 XF322 '962/HF', is seen here at Hal Far in 1960 or 1961 when overall HSS with yellow T-bands was still in style (just). Converted to T.8C standard in 1967 then allocated to 759 NAS in July that year, XF322 was operating from Brawdy when it was involved in a mid-air collision over the St George's Channel with XF938 on 15 December 1967; the crew of XF322 ejected safely although both were injured, while XF938's crew were both killed. *Tony Buttler collection*

RNAS Yeovilton, named HMS *Heron*, maintained its own station flight which became known as Heron Flight. Many aircraft types have served with the Flight including the Hunter T.7, T.8 and GA.11. Here T.8C, WV396 '748', is seen in September 1969 finished in overall HSS with day-glo panels and white-painted underwing tanks. The motif on the nose is a stylised heron on a small white cloud. Usually painted medium/dark blue, the heron appears to be black in this instance, although by mid-1971 it was most certainly blue. *Fred Martin collection*

# Royal Navy GA.11

GA.11, XE680 '789/BY'. Seen c1966, this is the leader of the 'Rough Diamonds' display team that was formed by 738 NAS at Brawdy in the summer of 1965 (until 1969). The team comprised four Hunters and all bar the leader's aircraft wore standard Extra Dark Sea Grey (EDSG) uppers over White under surfaces while the leader's aircraft featured a day-glo nose cone, spine and wingtips. 'Pegasus' appeared on both sides of the nose. *Tony Buttler collection*

In addition to the Hunter F.4 to T.8 conversions, the RN also received forty single-seat ex-F.4 to GA.11 conversions for use in the training role: ten unconverted F.4s were also acquired for ground instructional purposes. All forty GA.11 conversions retained their original 'small-bore' engines, had leading-edge wing extensions, TACAN, and an airfield arrester hook fitted, but only about sixteen of their number were equipped with the Mod. 228 four-pylon wing.

The Navy, seeing no apparent need for the Aden cannon had them removed, however, their GA.11s were wired to carry Bullpup and Sidewinder missiles as carried by the Navy's Scimitars and other front-line types, although doubt exists as to whether live rounds of either type were ever carried by Royal Navy Hunters.

After being phased out of service in their training role, surviving GA.11s (and PR.11s) were passed to the FRADU, the last being retired in 1995.

GA.11, XF977 '695/LM', from 764 NAS is seen wearing the standard colour scheme of the day, EDSG over White with the unit's markings on the nose (white scales on a black disc flanked by green and white checks). Having joined 764 at Lossiemouth in October 1962 coded '695/LM', XF977 became '691/LM' in February 1965. Twelve months later it was undergoing modernisation at Kemble where it likely received the PR nose seen here. Returned to the Squadron in September 1966, still coded '691', the latter changed to '696/LM' in early 1969. Transferred to FRADU in December 1972, XF977 crashed into the sea off Devon on 29 October 1980. *Newark Air Museum*

An otherwise anonymous GA.11 is seen on an undisclosed date, although there's a fighting chance that this is XE673 which was coded '680/LM' on arrival at 764 NAS in late 1970 and remained with the unit until flown to 5MU Kemble on 17 July 1972, ten days before 764 disbanded. The Squadron's markings are as described earlier, while White has replaced EDSG along the Hunter's spine.

FRADU GA.11, WV267 '836' ('VL' temporarily removed?), seen at Greenham Common in July 1977 wearing EDSG over White with the code '36' in black on the nosewheel door and a nose-mounted Harley light that had been fitted in October 1968. Photographs taken at this time reveal that WV267's port underwing tank was painted as per WT804's starboard tank (beyond). *Both: Fred Martin collection*

FRADU PR.11, WT723 '866/VL', seen at Yeovilton in August 1984 wearing EDSG over White. Following the Falklands War, a 'toning-down' policy was undertaken in which the latter scheme was replaced by overall glossy Dark Sea Grey (DSG) with two-colour Red/Blue national markings – as seen on the neighbouring Hunter.

FRADU GA.11, WT744 '868/LM', seen at Yeovilton in August 1977 wearing EDSG over White with a day-glo band around the circumference of its Harley light. Having served with 764 NAS as '692/LM' until mid-1972, WT744 spent the next few years in storage and on flight trials prior to being transferred to FRADU in February 1977. Still coded '692/LM' on arrival, the numeric code was soon changed to '868' although several months would pass before 'LM' (Lossiemouth) was altered to 'VL' (Yeovilton). *Both: Fred Martin collection*

A second image of FRADU GA.11, WT744 '868/VL', seen at Coningsby in June 1986 wearing overall glossy DSG with two-colour national markings – albeit by this time 'LM' had long since been replaced by 'VL'. As can be seen, this airframe was one of a relatively small number of GA.11s to be fitted with the Mod. 228 four-pylon wing. WT744 continued to fly until 16 March 1994, after which it was withdrawn from service and later sold. *Fred Martin collection*

FRADU GA.11, XF300 '860/LM', seen at Yeovilton in October 1988 and included purely to help illustrate the under surfaces of an overall DSG GA.11. Its service complete, XF300 was dispatched to Shawbury's storage unit on 12 June 1995 where it remained until sold almost six years later. *Fred Martin collection*

Slightly off the beaten track is GA.11, WT804 '831/DD' with XE668 '832/DD' beyond. Their flying days (seemingly) over, a few GA.11s continued to play a useful role with the School of Aircraft Handling at Culdrose, where this photo was taken in September 1985. Strictly, WT804 was now Ground (Training) Reserve B (GRB) airframe A2732/E4782 (A = airframe, E= engine). 'DD' on the tail very likely alludes to dummy deck training but does anyone remember 'Double Diamond' bitter? (probably best forgotten!) *Fred Martin collection*

# British Hunter Camouflage and Markings

Designed as a single-seat day fighter, all the first production models of the Hawker Hunter were finished on the production line in the then relatively newly introduced scheme for home-based day fighters, promulgated in December 1952, under Air Ministry Order A658/52, comprising glossy Dark Green and Dark Sea Grey upper surfaces, which was essentially based on the original Air Diagram for Single Engine Monoplanes, AD1160, to the B Scheme, with 'silver' under surfaces, which by the early 1950s was known as High-Speed Silver, to Pattern No 1, (where the upper surface colour demarcation was low on the fuselage sides),

The national markings comprised of 1-2-3 proportioned Bright Red, White and Bright Blue roundels, in all six positions, those above the wings being 48 inches in diameter with those on the fuselage sides and under the wings being 36 inches in diameter. The fin flash, comprising equally proportioned Bright Red, White and Bright Blue vertical stripes, was 21½ inches high and 18 inches in width positioned immediately above the tailplanes.

- **Post Office Red** (BS 381C 538) was used for national markings as well as ejection seat warning triangles etc.

- **Signal Red** (BS 381C 537) was used for aircraft colour schemes.

- **Aircraft Blue** (BS 381C 108) was used until 1965 for the blue portions of the national markings.

- **Roundel Blue** (BS 381C 110 was introduced in 1965 to replace Aircraft Blue (i.e., in national markings).

Hunter serial numbers were applied in black in 8in high characters on the rear fuselage beneath the tailplane, just above the upper/under surface camouflage demarcation line, while the underwing serials were 24in high, initially in a straight line running inboard from the underwing roundel across the undercarriage leg covers, reading from the front under the port wing and from the rear under the starboard wing. The fin top and nose tip dielectric panels were black, although they tended to fade to a brownish-black over time.

In the mid-1950s, many Hunter squadrons chose to display their respective unit colours by applying horizontal bars either side of their fuselage roundels, whereas others chose instead to apply stylised versions of their respective squadron motifs on the Hunter's nose – often, but not always, flanked by squadron bars of varying dimensions. Inevitably exceptions occurred whereby *both* forms were applied simultaneously by some units, while others switched from one style of presentation to the other. It was very fluid!

Initially, individual aircraft code letters were applied to the fuselage tail cone, but practical considerations quickly dictated a relocation to the fin. Generally the code letter was also repeated on the nosewheel door.

Occasionally, exercise markings were applied, usually to an area of the fin, in washable white distemper – e.g. as seen on 74 Squadron's Hunter F.4s during Exercise *Vigilant*, a defence exercise to test the RAF's ability to intercept attacks on RAF and USAF bases in the UK in May 1957.

**The Suez Crisis**
The F.5 became the first Hunter variant to see combat when 1 and 34 Squadrons were deployed against the Egyptians during Operation *Musketeer* – the Suez Crisis of October/November 1956. Despite confidence that the Hunter would be a match for the Egyptian MiG-15s and MiG-17s, no such confrontation occurred. In fact, other than a few patrols over the Canal Zone, the type's lack of range and the Egyptian lack of opposition, meant they were consigned to guarding the packed airfields on Cyprus against a threat from Egyptian Il-28 'Beagle' bombers.

The only change in the standard markings for *Musketeer* was that two 12in-wide black, and three alternating 12in-wide yellow 'Suez Stripes' were applied around the wings and rear fuselage, although due to a shortage of the official BS 381C 356 Yellow at RAF Nicosia at that time, it is thought that either household emulsion paint or perhaps more likely a simple mix of Yellow and BS 381C 302 White was used to create the 'cream' colour that most RAF aircraft based at Nicosia used throughout the Crisis. Although the underwing serial numbers were invariably painted over, the roundels were either avoided or carefully painted around.

By the time the Hunter F.6 entered service in late 1956, the only major change to occur was the repositioning of the underwing serial numbers, whereby the two prefix letters were placed above the numerals, effectively creating two rows, again positioned across the undercarriage leg covers, and reading from the front under the port wing and from the rear under the starboard wing. Additionally, some Hunters were seen with white fuselage serial numbers, initially introduced in 1958 for camouflaged aircraft, although the practice doesn't appear to have been adopted universally, and throughout the type's service, Hunters were seen with either white, or black, fuselage serial numbers.

**Ground Attack and Fighter Reconnaissance roles**
Light Aircraft Grey under surfaces were introduced to replace the High-Speed Silver undersides from the early/mid-1960s, by which time the Hunter had been relieved of its pure day fighter role (by the English Electric Lightning – see Flight Craft 11) but was given a new lease of life in the operational training and ground support role.

Remaining F.6s, and the FGA.9s, initially retained an overall gloss finish, but by the late 1960s/early 1970s, an overall matt finish was being introduced and a softer edge to the camouflage was, by now, commonly seen. Additional to the matt finish, a general toning-down of national markings was also being introduced to operational training and ground support aircraft from the early 1970s, with Red and Blue roundels replacing the Red/White/Blue roundels on the wing upper surfaces and fuselage sides and Red/Blue fin flashes replacing the Red/White/Blue ones – all to the same diameters and dimensions as the previous markings – whereas the underwing roundels generally remained Red/White/Blue.

It was in this general scheme of matt camouflage colours and toned-down national markings that the Hunter saw out its frontline operational service with the RAF.

**Training Schemes**
Most readers will be aware that the majority of RAF-operated single-seat Hunters shared similarities in external appearance in terms of camouflage, unit codes and unit 'heraldry' for decades – to the extent that one might reasonably consider that they invariably conformed more or less to a uniform or 'standard' appearance. (Readers will also be aware, having reached this point in the book, that it is most unwise to use the word 'invariably' when discussing the Hunter!)

With the Hunter T.7, however, colour variations abounded. Initially the majority of T.7s were finished in overall High-Speed Silver (HSS) with Yellow 24in wide, identification bands around the rear fuselage and both surfaces of the mainplanes just outboard of the engine intakes, which were generally termed 'Trainer' or 'T-Bands'. Red, White and Blue roundels were carried in all six positions with Red, White and Blue fin flashes.

Nevertheless, by 1963, the Yellow T-Bands had largely been replaced following the introduction of day-glo paint or day-glo stick-on strips. At a later date overall Light Aircraft Grey (LAG) replaced HSS to which day-glo strips or day-glo paint, or both, were applied, while later still Signal Red BS 381C 537 was also used, although the precise sequence and chronology of their introduction is a little uncertain. (*Should any reader be in possession of the facts, the authors would be delighted to hear from them via the Publisher. Such information would be of great benefit for forthcoming titles*.)

In the early 1970s, a new high-visibility Fixed Wing Training-Aircraft Scheme consisting of LAG, Signal Red and White was introduced by the RAF. It was soon applied to the Hunter F.6s and T.7s used by 4 Flying Training School that had joined the syllabus in 1967; prior to which the F.6s had, in essence, retained their original camouflage colours while most, if not all, of their T.7s were finished in LAG with day-glo bands and/or stripes. Having emerged from the paintshop in their new colours, each 4 FTS Hunter now displayed a Signal Red/White fuselage, Light Aircraft Grey wings (with Signal Red wing tips), a White tail and Signal Red tailplanes.

The majority of operational Hunter squadrons also acquired one, sometimes two, T.7s for pilot appraisal, instrument rating and continuity training. Initially most wore the standard Trainer Scheme of overall HSS with Yellow T-bands, but with time they and others that were operated by RAF OCUs and other second-line units transitioned to a camouflage scheme of Dark Green and Dark Sea Grey upper surfaces and Light Aircraft Grey under surfaces.

By the late 1970s, lo-viz toned-down Red/Blue national markings were being applied, and several of the remaining T.7s that survived into the late 1980s and beyond, received a matt overall/wraparound Dark Green/Dark Sea Grey camouflage scheme that was being applied to ground attack and tactical strike/reconnaissance aircraft such as Harriers, Jaguars and Buccaneers at the time.

In 1991, Air Chief Marshal Sir Patrick Hine, GCB, GBE, retired from the RAF, and to honour him four two-seat Hunters were painted overall matt black to commemorate his time as a pilot with the famous 'Black Arrows' of 111 Squadron. The airframes were WV318, XL568, XL614 and XL616.

Many Hunters of several Marks were operated by specialist units such as the RAE, ETPS and A&AEE who often applied striking colour schemes to their airframes. The colour schemes employed evolved and changed across the years within these (and other) establishments, the best known of which, arguably, was the so-called 'Raspberry Ripple' scheme consisting of Signal Red, White and Oxford Blue (BS 381C 105).

**OCU and TWU 'reserve/Reserve' Squadrons**
In early 1959, 229 OCU at Chivenor very likely became the first unit to feature (otherwise redundant) squadron markings on their Hunters, notably the 'on paper-only' reserve units 145 and 234 Squadrons. As with frontline Hunter units, considerable variation existed in the presentation of their 'heraldry'. Squadron bars might be found on either side of the fuselage roundels; on either side of a squadron motif on the nose and occasionally (on some T.7s) aft of the cockpit. Alternatively no such 'heraldry' need appear at all. Certainly in 229 OCU's case, several of its Hunters carried one of two unit codes ('ES' or 'RS'), but only until they were dispensed with c1960. Perhaps the only relatively consistent marking was the airframe's individual code number (or letter) on the fin, often to be found repeated on the nosewheel door.

The individual codes were also OCU fleet numbers/letters. They were applied in various colours in a bewildering variety of styles, often, but certainly not invariably, on a yellow disc. The situation didn't really alter very much after 229 OCU evolved into the TWU on 2 September 1974, on which day 63, 79 and 234 Squadrons formally became Reserve squadrons - hence 63[R], 79[R] and 234[R] Squadrons respectively.

*Please refer to Appendix 2, Note 1, for an explanation concerning 'shadow/reserve/Reserve' squadrons*

**Royal Navy/Fleet Air Arm colour schemes**
The Fleet Air Arm (FAA) was also a prolific user of the Hunter, in both single and twin-seat versions, albeit with different designations.

Initially painted in glossy Extra Dark Sea Grey upper surfaces with White undersides, Red/White/Blue roundels were carried in all six positions with the 4in high serial number and 8in high ROYAL NAVY lettering on the rear fuselage in white and the 24in high underwing serial presentation in black. The two-letter RN Air Station identification code was usually applied to the fin in white, with a three-digit numerical code on the nose also in white.

From the mid-1980s, GA.11s serving with the FRADU were repainted in overall gloss Dark Sea Grey and had toned-down Red/Blue roundels applied. The previously white identification markings such as the serial number, ROYAL NAVY lettering, two-letter RN Air Station identification code and the three-digit numerical code on the nose were re-applied in black.

The Royal Navy's twin-seat Hunters, like their RAF cousins, started their service lives in overall High-Speed Silver with Red, White and Blue roundels carried in all six positions but no fin flashes. Serial number presentation was similar to that used by the RAF, in black, but the actual serial number was often in a reduced 4in high format with the legend ROYAL NAVY, 8 inches high, immediately above it like the single-seaters. Some aircraft carried Yellow T-bands but from the early 1960s, fluorescent day-glo bands were applied, again with additional narrower day-glo bands on the nose and often the rear fuselage. Variations in the day-glo presentations, which also included alternative gloss fluorescent reds and oranges, were applied to several Brawdy, Lossiemouth and Yeovilton-based T.8s in the form of shaped 'panels' under the nose, on the rear fuselage spine and fin, and in broad triangles on both surfaces of the wings.

In the late 1960s/early 1970s, the T.8's basic airframe colour was changed to overall gloss Light Aircraft Grey, with day-glo panels on the upper and lower wing surfaces, fin and nose. Then in the mid-1980s, the T.8s that were passed to the FRADU were painted overall gloss Dark Sea Grey and had toned-down Red/Blue roundels applied, like the unit's GA.11s. Similarly, the serial number, ROYAL NAVY lettering, two-letter RN Air Station identification code and the three-digit numerical code on the nose were re-applied in black.

**Aerobatic Display Team schemes**
When 111 Squadron exchanged its Hunter F.4s for F.6s in November 1956, it was invited to form an aerobatic team to fly at air displays. Known as the 'Black Arrows', their Hunters were repainted in an overall glossy black finish, with standard Red, White and Blue roundels in all six positions. Although a 2in white border was applied to the national markings, the photo of F.6 XG203 (q.v.), taken in early 1957, implies that the white surround was a later addition. No underwing serials were carried but red 4in high serials were applied to the rear fuselage and a red 8in high individual aircraft letter was carried on the nosewheel door. A miniature version of 111 Squadron's badge in a standard frame, flanked by the Squadron bars, was carried on the port side of the nose with the pilot's name above it.

In 1960, 92 Squadron, under the command of Squadron Leader Brian Mercer – who had been a Flight Commander with 'Treble One' – was chosen as Fighter Command's official RAF Aerobatic Display Team, taking over from the 'Black Arrows' in 1961. Initially named 'The Falcons' the team soon adopted the name 'Blue Diamonds' when the aircraft were repainted overall in BS 381C 108 Aircraft Blue, with the standard Red, White and Blue roundels in all six positions having white 1in wide surrounds, as did the 'angled' fin flash. Again, no underwing serials were carried but black 2in high serial numbers were applied to the rear fuselage. Individual aircraft letters, also 2 inches high in black, were applied above the fin flash and repeated 8 inches high in white on the nosewheel door. The 'Blue Diamonds' aerobatic team aircraft featured a modified 92 Squadron motif in which the Cobra's head was enlarged and appeared with only one red maple leaf, not two as previously. The motif was still flanked by the Squadron's red and yellow checked bars, thinly outlined in black, on both sides of the nose with a white 'lightning bolt' running down the full length of the fuselage. The wing tips were also white.

The 'Rough Diamonds' was the Royal Navy's FAA aerobatic display team which formed in the summer of 1965. The team, (which apparently got the name from the shape of the Hunter), flew four Hunter GA.11s from 738 NAS based at RNAS Brawdy.

All four display team aircraft, plus the 'spare', were finished in the standard FAA colour scheme of glossy Extra Dark Sea Grey upper surfaces with White undersides and carried standard Red/White/Blue roundels in all six positions. The white 4in high serial number and 8in high ROYAL NAVY lettering were carried on the rear fuselage, with the underwing serial presentation 24 inches high in black. The two-letter RN Air Station identification code, 'BY' for Brawdy, was applied to the fin in white, with the three-digit numerical code on the nose also in white. The team's leader, Lt Cdr Christopher Comins' aircraft had a day-glo red nose-band, fuselage spine and wing tips. The 'Rough Diamonds' display team was disbanded in 1969.

The 'Blue Herons' was the Navy's other aerobatic display team that flew Hunters, albeit manned by civilian pilots contracted by Airwork Services Ltd for the Fleet Requirements and Air Direction Unit (FRADU). A four-aircraft display team, formed in 1975, they first displayed on 6 September that year at RNAS Yeovilton's Air Day and then continued to perform at numerous airshows. With their outstanding formation flying, they won trophies at the International Air Tattoos of 1976 and 1977 and continued to display until the winter of 1980 when the team was disbanded due to FRADU's busy work schedule of providing simulated ship attacks, airborne early warning fighter controller training and helicopter fighter affiliation training with Hunters, Canberras and Sea Vixens.

As with the 'Rough Diamonds', the Hunters were finished in the standard FAA colour scheme of glossy Extra Dark Sea Grey upper surfaces with White undersides and carried standard national markings and serials. At least seven GA.11s were used by the team during its existence, WT804/831, WT806/838, WT809/867, WV267/836, WW654/833, XE668/832, XE682/835 and one PR.11, XF977/865, but only WT804/831 appears to have carried the two-letter RN Air Station identification code, 'VL' for Yeovilton, applied to the fin.

The name 'Blue Herons' became the first aerobatic display team in the world whereby civilian pilots flew military aircraft. The 'Blue Herons' were briefly reformed in 1984 and 1986 for displays at RNAS Yeovilton and at RNAS Culdrose Air Days.

**Hunter second prototype, WB195, Kingston-upon-Thames, May 1952** | WB195 first flew on 5th May 1952 and, unlike the first prototype WB188, was equipped with a full Aden gun and radar ranging installation. The aircraft was involved in a number of the trials aimed at correcting the P.1067's initial shortcomings. As a result WB195 was used for spinning and airbrake development trials and for experiments to correct the buffeting experienced around the tail/tailplane junction. This resulted in WB195 being fitted with the extended fin fillet seen here. Also note the longer and more bulbous design of the spine aft of the cockpit and the shorter sliding hood of the first two prototypes. Due to criticisms of the aircraft's limited rearward visibility the spine was slimmed down and the canopy transparency extended aft by around a foot. The new design was incorporated into the third prototype, WB202, but WB188 and WB195 retained the original design seen here. In common with WB188, WB195 was painted in a unique gloss 'Duck Egg Green' shade custom developed for and donated to Hawker by Cellon Ltd.

**Hunter F.1, WT695 'N', 233 Operational Conversion Unit, RAF Pembrey, 1956** | 233 OCU, based at Pembrey in south-west Wales, operated fifteen Hunter F.1s. Initially operated by 229 OCU at Chivenor, WT695 moved to 233 OCU before ultimately succumbing to the scrapman at Kemble in April 1958. The aircraft wears the standard camouflage pattern of Dark Green and Dark Sea Grey uppers, with High Speed Silver (HSS) under surfaces. The outer wing panels were painted yellow to aid visibility. Standard black 8-inch-high serials were carried on the rear fuselage with the individual code letter presented in yellow on the rear fuselage repeated in black on the nosewheel door. WT695 has been retrofitted with link collectors, although it lacks the extended cartridge chutes fitted to later Hunters. Hunters were prone to staining on their rear fuselage from the engine cooling outlets and lubrication system, for this reason many units relocated their unit or squadron bars from the centre of the fuselage roundel to a position level with the top of it.

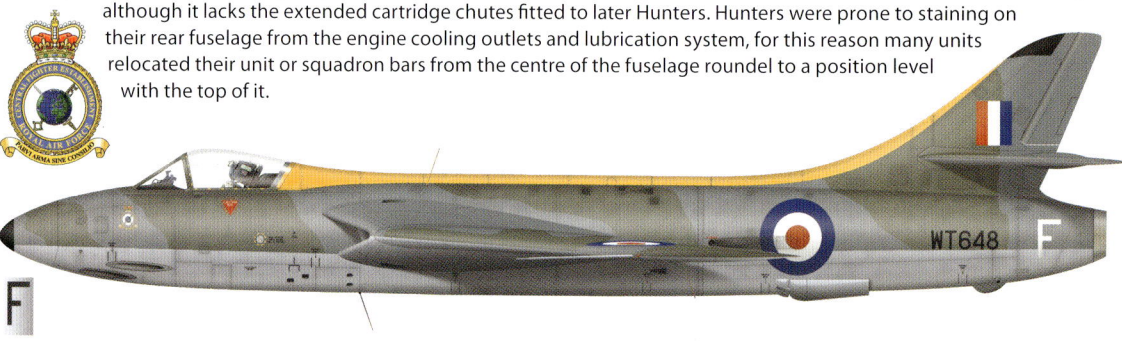

**Hunter F.1, WT648 'F', Day Fighter Leaders School, RAF West Raynham, 1955** | WT648 was delivered to 222 Sqn in November 1954 but moved to the DFLS, part of the Central Fighter Establishment shortly afterwards. WT648 later became 7530M at RAF St Athan and the privately-owned cockpit section survives to this day at the Boscombe Down Museum. Finished in the standard Dark Green/Dark Sea Grey/High Speed Silver (DG/DSG/HSS) scheme with the serial number in black, the individual code was white repeated in black on the nosewheel door. The DFLS operated two Flights, 'A' (red) and 'B' (yellow), the spine and fin leading edge being colour-coded accordingly. Other publications have described this aircraft as having a white spine but the surviving cockpit section has remains of yellow paint in that area, as illustrated. The early practice of placing the code on the removable tail cone was quickly discontinued as it caused significant problems when servicing, tail cones, and thus codes, often being swapped between aircraft. The badge of the CFE is believed to have been carried on the side of the nose.

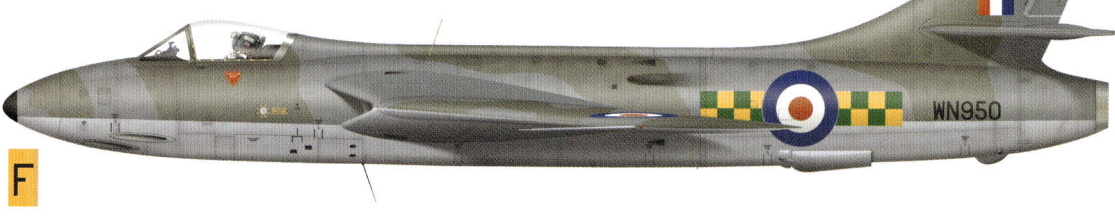

**Hunter F.2, WN950 'F', 257 Sqn, RAF Wattisham, 1955** | 257 Sqn was the first receive the Sapphire-powered Hunter F.2. The unit's green and yellow checks, initially carried on the rear fuselage, were later moved to the nose along with the chinthe from the unit's badge. WN950 wears the standard DG/DSG/HSS scheme with the serial in black and the individual code in yellow on the fin; the code being repeated in black on a yellow background on the nosewheel door. Note the original positioning of the cartridge ejection ports prior to the introduction of the link collectors.

**Hunter F.1, WT695 'N', 233 Operational Conversion Unit, RAF Pembrey, 1956** | These illustrations show the standard disruptive camouflage pattern applied to RAF single-engined monoplanes of the time. This pattern, finished in Dark Green and Dark Sea Grey was retained for all camouflaged Hunters throughout the type's service, the only modification being the switch from DG/DSG with HSS undersides to Light Aircraft Grey (LAG) undersides in the mid-1960s. In common with a number of units, 233 OCU added their own embellishments to the standard scheme; yellow outer wing panels in this case. At this time underwing serials were applied as a single line of characters although this would subsequently alter to become a double line with the introduction of underwing stores. [Compare with F.6 XG199]

**Hunter F.4, WT720 'Q', 111 Sqn, RAF North Weald, 1956** | 'Treble One' Sqn, of Black Arrows fame, operated Hunter F.4s at North Weald between June 1955 and November 1956. On 10th September 1956, WT720 gained the dubious distinction of becoming the first Hunter to land on two wheels when the starboard main undercarriage leg remained firmly locked up, despite which, Flying Officer Michael Thurley skilfully brought WT720 back to earth with minimal damage. The unit's distinctive black and yellow squadron bars are carried on the rear fuselage with matching individual code (repeated in black on the nosewheel door) on the forward part of the fin. Camouflage scheme is the standard DG/DSG/HSS, but wing tips are red and a small Union Flag is displayed below the windscreen.

**Hunter F.4 XE665, 122 Wing, RAF Jever, 1956** | XE665 was the first of two F.4s to be used by Jever's Wing Leader, Wg Cdr C. S. 'Hammer' West, the second being XF315 which replaced XE665 when the aircraft was transferred to 118 Sqn in April 1956. XE665's special markings consisted of miniature versions of the insignia of 4, 93, 98 and 118 Squadrons, the units making up 122 Wing, and a red/yellow check pattern on the nosewheel door. Apart from the Wing Commander's rank pennant, the aircraft featured the standard DG/DSG/HSS camouflage pattern, with yellow stencilled emergency and warning notices repeated in German on the nose. Converted to a T.8, it was sold into civilian ownership in 1995.

**Hunter F.4, XF295 'C', 130 Sqn, RAF Bruggen, 1956** | 130 Sqn was one of many Hunter units based in Germany although it operated Hunters for only thirteen months from April 1956. XF295 displays typical markings including the unit's colourful bars and elephant's head (which faced forward on the left side of the aircraft). The colour of the disc on the fin containing the individual code letter identified the aircraft's flight allocation (red for 'A' Flight, blue for 'B' Flight) which, in this case, is outlined in white to signify its use by the CO.

**Hunter F.4, WW663 'H', 14 Sqn, RAF Oldenburg, 1957** | 14 Sqn received its first Hunters (F.4s) at Oldenburg in May 1955, with F.6s arriving in April 1957 to coincide with a move to RAF Ahlhorn, Germany. WW663 was the personal mount of the unit's CO, Sqn Ldr R. S. Kingsford, and carried the appropriate rank pennant on the side of the nose below the canopy. Unusually the rear portion of the tail cone was unpainted. While this was common practice in some air forces, e.g. the Royal Netherlands Air Force, it was very unusual for RAF Hunters and seems to have been confined to a small number of Germany-based 2 TAF F.4s. The fibreglass IFF aerial panel atop the fin is, in this instance, coloured light grey rather than the more usual black.

**Hunter F.4, WT748 'S', 118 Sqn, RAF Jever, 1957** | Speculation exists over the possibility that some RAF Germany Hunters were painted with PRU Blue undersides. A handful of photographs exist which appear to show darker undersides on a small number of aircraft. One particular image of WT748 next to another Hunter shows the contrast between their undersides very clearly, supporting the idea that it was indeed PRU Blue underneath. Eye-witness evidence from a number of sources also back up the theory. This illustration is based on that photo, taken at Bruggen in mid-1957.

**Hunter F.4, WW650 'R', 222 Sqn, RAF Leuchars, 1957** | 222 Sqn converted to the Hunter F.1 in December 1954 and re-equipped with the F.4 in August 1956. As has been noted, due to staining on the rear fuselage from the engine cooling outlets and lubrication system, many units moved their squadron bars to a position level with the top of the fuselage roundel. WW650 joined 222 Squadron in May 1957 following two years with 98 Squadron, by which time the individual code, in white, had been relocated from the tail cone to a position atop the fin and was repeated in black on the nosewheel door.

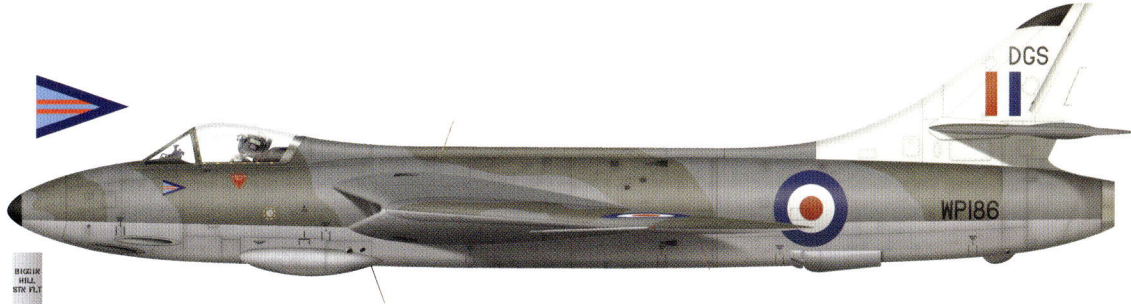

**Hunter F.5 WP186 'DGS', Station Flight, RAF Biggin Hill, 1955** | WP186 was the personal aircraft of Biggin Hill Station Commander Wing Commander Denis G. Smallwood, later Air Chief Marshall Sir Dennis Graham Smallwood, GBE, KCB, DSO, DFC, FRAeS, FRSA. In addition to the standard camouflage scheme of DG/DSG/HSS, the aircraft sports a white painted fin with Wg Cdr Smallwood's initials in black. The nosewheel door carries the stencilled inscription 'Biggin Hill Stn Flt' in black and the Wing Commander's rank pennant is displayed below the windscreen.

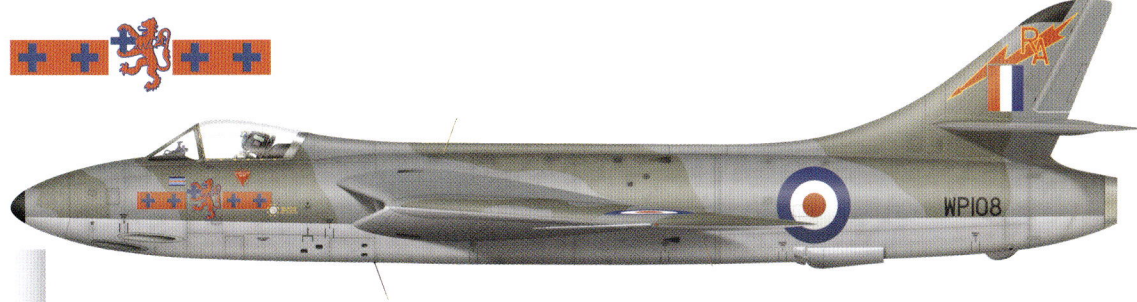

**Hunter F.5, WP108 'RA', 263 Sqn, RAF Wattisham, 1956** | 263 Sqn supplemented its Hunter F.2s with F.5s in 1955 with WP108 becoming the personal aircraft of the OC, Sqn Ldr R Aytoun. As such, WP108 carried a thunderbolt/arrow on the fin with the OC's initials superimposed as the individual code; both in red outlined in yellow. Ordinarily 263 Sqn Hunters had the code repeated in red on the nosewheel door, but WP108 appears not to have followed suit. The unit's distinctive bars and 'lion rampant holding in its forepaws a cross' emblem is carried on the nose, the design of which was later modified to include a fine yellow outline. The lion, facing forward on both sides of the aircraft, represented the unit's association with Scotland, while the cross, from the flag of Norway, celebrates the unit's exploits in that country in 1940.

**Hunter F.6, XE593 'P', 65 Sqn, RAF Duxford, May 1957** | XE593 is illustrated here as it appeared on 25th May 1957, the first day of Exercise *Vigilant*. The three-day exercise was designed to test Fighter Command's defences against 400-500 'raiders', including RAF V-bombers, USAF B-45s and B-57s, various Fleet Air Arm aircraft and French Air Force Mystères. Defending by day were Hunters from a number of squadrons and by night Gloster Javelins of 23 and 141 Sqns. 'Home' aircraft were identified by a temporary white-painted fin as worn by XE593. Otherwise the colour scheme is the standard disruptive pattern with HSS undersides and white wing tips. A slightly italicised code letter is carried on the fin in yellow and repeated in white with a thin red outline on the nosewheel door with the squadron markings adorning the nose.

**Hunter F.6, XG239 'MH', 92 Sqn, RAF Hal Far, 1958** | Following delivery in November 1956, XG239 was issued to 92 Squadron and became the personal mount of Sqn Ldr Mike Hobson. During an Armament Practice Camp (APC) in Cyprus in January 1958, the aircraft crashed after take-off from Nicosia, Hobson survived the incident but XG239 was destroyed. Well known for the Blue Diamonds aerobatic display team, XG239 represents 92 Squadron's Hunters in a less flamboyant colour scheme. White wing tips embellish the standard camouflage pattern along with a chequerboard pattern in the 92 Squadron colours of yellow and red at the base of the fin. These are repeated, along with the unit's cobra and maple leaf insignia on the nose.

**Hunter F.6, XG266 'R', 66 Sqn, RAF Acklington, 1958** | XG266 was operated by 66 Sqn between December 1956 and November 1960 and is shown here wearing the usual DG/DSG/HSS scheme with white wing tips. Less common is the raked fin flash which was a feature of many 66 Squadron Hunters. The white with blue outline squadron markings are prominent on the rear fuselage and the unit badge is presented on a white disc thinly outlined in black on the nose. The individual code appears in white on the fin and is repeated in black on the nosewheel door.

**Hunter F.6. XG199 'J', 19 Sqn, RAF Church Fenton, 1961** | Delivered to 33MU in October 1956 and subsequently to 19 Sqn and 229 OCU, XG199 is still extant and displayed at the *Museo Nacional Aeronáutico y del Espacio* in Santiago, Chile. During its time with 19 Sqn, XG199 wore the standard camouflage scheme with HSS undersides and white wing tips shown here, the serial and individual codes are displayed in white, with the code repeated in blue on the nosewheel door. The unit's blue and white checks are repeated in miniature straddling the Squadron badge on the nose. Note the blue lightning bolts displayed on the ends of the wing tips. A non-standard pattern, soft-edged area of Dark Green camouflage on the nose suggests an area repainted at some stage.

**Hunter F.6, XG199 'J', 19 Squadron, RAF Church Fenton, 1961** | These views illustrate the standard disruptive pattern applied throughout the service life of the Hunter – Dark Green/Dark Sea Grey upper surfaces with High Speed Silver undersides. A few years later (in the mid-1960s) the underside colour was changed to Light Aircraft Grey, a colour notoriously difficult to distinguish from High Speed Silver (especially when worn or dirty) in black and white photographs. Note the revised presentation of the underwing serial numbers using two lines of characters compared to F.1 WT695 illustrated earlier. This was necessary to avoid the serial being obscured when carrying underwing stores.

**Hunter F.6, XG236 'N', 66 Sqn (on temporary loan to the Royal Iraqi Air Force), 1957** | XG236 was issued to 66 Sqn at RAF Linton-on-Ouse in November 1956. In May 1957, while detached to RAF Akrotiri, the aircraft was one of two selected to have Iraqi markings applied and to be temporarily loaned to the RIAF. With the US having funded a number of Hunters for King Faisal II's air force, a celebratory flypast, to include all the new aircraft, was arranged in Baghdad. To ensure a full complement of Hunters, F.6s XG236 and XG251 were repainted with Iraqi markings (but retained RAF serials) and dispatched from Cyprus to Baghdad to be held in reserve in case of serviceability issues with the Iraqi aircraft. In the event neither were required and they returned shortly afterwards to 66 Sqn. Note the aircraft has yet to receive the Mod. 228 'dog tooth' wings or gun blast deflectors which were to become characteristic features of the F.6.

**Hunter F.6, XG257 'C', 93 Sqn, RAF Jever, 1960** | 93 Sqn received its F.6s in March 1957 with XG257 arriving in January 1960. XG257 wears the standard DG/DSG/HSS scheme with the addition of yellow wing tips. In common with many RAFG Hunters, safety-related stencilling is repeated in German on the forward fuselage. With the switch from the F.4 to the F.6 came the relocation of the unit's arrowhead markings from the rear fuselage to the nose in a smaller size and flanking a yellow escarbuncle on a blue background. The pilot's name, in this case 'Flt. Lt. Mick Ryan', and '93 Squadron' were stencilled in the same colours above and below the Squadron markings. A Union Flag was also applied to both sides of the nose. The individual code is presented in yellow with a thin blue outline on the fin and repeated in yellow on the blue nosewheel door.

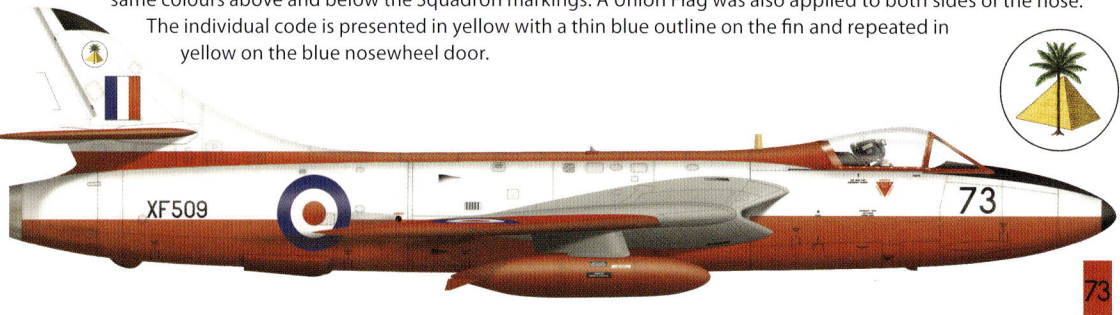

**Hunter F.6, XF509 '73', 4 Flying Training School, 1973** | XF509 was first issued to 54 Sqn before moving to Bristol to act as a chase-plane for the Fairey FD.2 programme in April 1963. After periods with a number of RAF squadrons, XF509 arrived at 4 FTS in 1968. The aircraft wears the scheme adopted for all training aircraft in the early 1970s of red and white fuselage, with red outer and LAG inner wings. The individual code is displayed below the windscreen and repeated on the nose gear door. The unit emblem of a pyramid and palm tree, commemorating the School's formation at Abu Sueir, Egypt in 1921, is worn atop the fin.

**Hunter F.6, XG185 '74', 4 Flying Training School, RAF Valley (date unknown)** | XG185 served with 3 and 19 Squadrons before being placed in storage with 5MU at RAF Kemble. Later issued to 4 FTS, XG185 was written off in April 1976. The standard colour scheme illustrated here includes the LAG undersides introduced in the mid-1960s. Note also the softer edge to the camouflage pattern and the 'wrap-around' along the wing leading edges. The black individual number appears on white discs on the fin and below the windscreen and was repeated on the nosewheel door. The nose also features a prominent arrowhead in day-glo, although its significance is unknown.

**Hunter F.6A, XG226 '28', 1 Tactical Weapons Unit, RAF Brawdy, c1980** | During the early 1980s four TWU Hunters were painted in a high-visibility scheme with coloured panels over their standard camouflage. XF418 '16' received red panels, XG172 '23' white, XG225 '27' yellow and XG226 '28' illustrated here, day-glo. The reasons for this are a little unclear as it has previously been thought they were used to more easily identify 'bounce' aircraft during training exercises. However, those that were at Brawdy at this time suggest they were part of high-visibility trials initiated following the mid-air collision of a Hunter and a 208 Squadron Buccaneer in 1977 resulting in the loss of the latter. Further concerns about the visibility of the smaller Hawk, at low-level and in the standard DG/DSG camouflage scheme, further prompted the trials. The Hawks were subsequently painted in overall gloss black however, which was found to provide the best visibility in most conditions.

**Hunter F.6A, XF382 '15', 79 Squadron, 1 TWU, RAF Brawdy, 1982** | Converted to F.6A standard, XF382 was later fitted with the oblique camera nose shown here. This modification, containing a single F95 camera, first appeared in the late 1960s when small numbers of Hunters were given a basic PR capability. Though lacking the full features of the FR.10, the camera could be effectively aimed by the pilot lining up the target with the top of the starboard wing tank. Just how many Hunters were modified in this way is unknown, but they have been noted with 20 Squadron, 1 TWU, 45 and 58 Squadrons. They were used for ad hoc PR duties in Aden, monitoring of Soviet shipping by Gibraltar-based Hunters, and by Brawdy-based aircraft in anti-smuggling and interdiction roles in the Irish Sea. Note the LAG undersides, 'wrap-around' wing leading edge camouflage, and low visibility national markings.

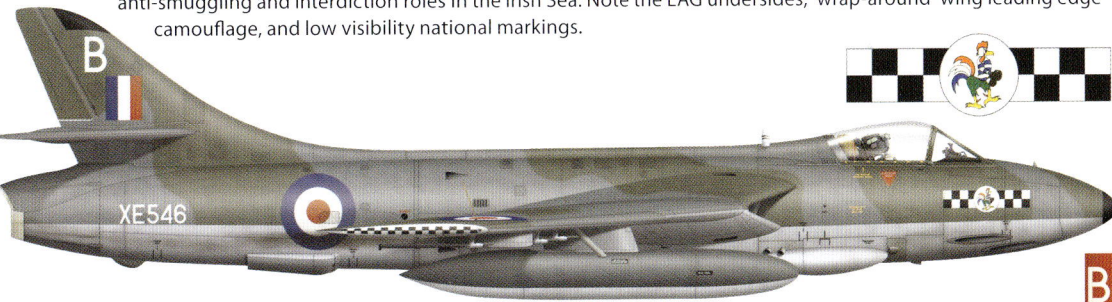

**Hunter FGA.9, XE546 'B', 43 Sqn, RAF Khormaksar, 1963** | 43 (Fighter) Squadron, the 'Fighting Cocks', was the first RAF squadron to operate the Hunter and continued to do so through all the major Marks. XE546 joined the unit in February 1962 and was later allocated to the CO of the joint 8 and 43 Squadron. The Squadron's famous black and white checks are prominently displayed on the nose straddling the stylised fighting cock emblem and are repeated on the wing tips. Note the empty Mk. 12 RP rails under the wings and, in common with many Hunters operating over potentially hostile territory, the presence of 'Survival Pack A' strapped behind the seat.

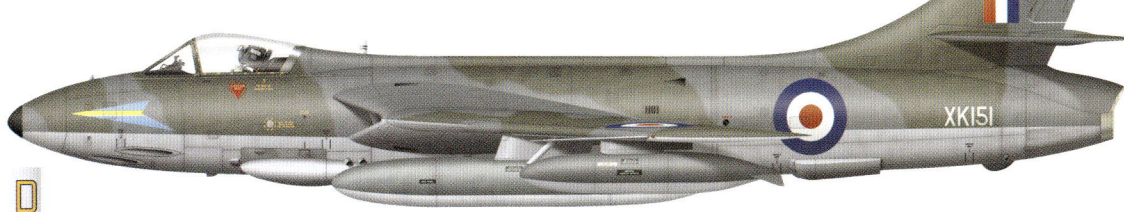

**Hunter FGA.9, XK151 'D', 208 Sqn, RAF Khormaksar, 1964** | XK151 was the last single-seat Hunter to be delivered to the RAF and, as a modified F.6, was one of two (the other being XK150) to take part in the Venom Replacement Evaluation Trials in Aden in August 1958. Having seen off the Folland Gnat, the Hunter FGA.9 became the RAF's preferred ground-attack aircraft and the replacement for the Venom. XK151 was thus returned to Hawker, upgraded to full FGA.9 standard and delivered into squadron service in January 1960. As with most 208 Squadron Hunters, the serial number is white with the individual aircraft letter in yellow on the fin and repeated with a thin black outline on the nosewheel door. The aircraft is illustrated in ferry configuration with both 230- and 100-gallon tanks fitted.

**Hunter FGA.9, XJ690 'G', 20 Sqn, RAF Tengah, 1966** | Delivered to 20 Sqn in October 1964, XJ690 is illustrated during the unit's annual APC at RAAF Butterworth in June/July 1966 carrying 12 x 3-inch RPs with 60 lb warheads which, apart from modifications to the mounting system, could trace their origins back to WW II. The DG/DSG/HSS scheme is enhanced by 20 Sqn's attractive markings on the nose, of which the rising sun commemorates the unit's long association with the East, while the Talwar sword, upon which the eagle is perched, with their historical links with the Army in India. The individual code is presented in white and repeated, with a thin black outline, on the red nosewheel door.

**Hunter FGA.9, XG296 'B', 8 and 43 Squadrons, RAF Khormaksar, 1967** | Between 1963 and 1967, 43 Squadron joined forces with 8 and 208 Squadrons and also 1417 Flight to form the Aden Strike Wing. Towards the end of their deployment 8 and 43 Squadrons shared aircraft which resulted in combined markings, with 43 Squadron's black and white checks aft of the fuselage roundel and 8 Squadron's yellow-blue-red stripes forward of it. White wing tips were also prominent. The combination of baking sun and abrasive sand meant that many Hunters based in the region looked faded and worn with the upper surface colours often becoming very patchy. A brown canvas 'Survival Pack A' is located behind the seat headbox, while a second smaller pack, ('Survival Pack B') was located on the starboard cockpit side wall.

**Hunter FGA.9, XJ642 'L', 54 Sqn, RAF West Raynham, 1968** | In 1960, 54 Sqn was transferred to the ground-attack role using FGA.9s which were retained until September 1969. Hunter Mod 1257 introduced the ability to carry RP launchers on the outer pylons and the aircraft is illustrated here carrying Matra Type 155 pods. The Type 155 launcher was loaded with 18 x 68mm SNEB rockets which could be configured, during pre-flight preparations, to fire individually or as a single ripple salvo with a 33-millisecond delay between each rocket's departure.

**Hunter FGA.9, XF430 'N', Harrier Conversion Team, RAF Wittering, 1969** | The Harrier Conversion Team, soon renamed Harrier Conversion Unit (and later resurrected as 233 OCU) was formed in January 1969 to convert pilots onto the then new Harrier GR.1. The unit operated a number of Hunters with XF430 being one of the first which, as an F.6, had once operated with 'Treble One' Sqn as a famed 'Black Arrow'. Converted to FGA.9 standard, XF430 was returned to RAF service in July 1965. The standard camouflage scheme is embellished only by the yellow individual letter on the fin, repeated in black on the nosewheel door, red wing tips and the 'Harrier Conversion Team' title in white on the nose.

HAWKER HUNTER IN COLOUR 75

**Hunter FGA.9, XG252 '87', 58 Sqn, RAF Wittering, 1976** | Reformed in 1973, 58 Sqn's primary role, and that of co-located 45 Sqn, was to train ground-attack pilots in preparation for the arrival of the Jaguar GR.1 which entered RAF squadron service in April 1974. XG252 is illustrated as it appeared just before being transferred to the TWU at Brawdy following 58 Squadron's disbandment in June 1976. The soft-edged DG/DSG upper surface disruptive scheme wrapped around the wing leading edges, LAG undersides and low visibility national markings typifies the final appearance of the camouflaged Hunter in RAF service.

**Hunter FR.10, XE589 'V', 8 Sqn, RAF Khormaksar, Kuwait Crisis, 1961** | Converted to FR.10 standard and delivered to 8 Sqn early in 1961, XE589, while based at Khormaksar, had the white bands seen here applied. Their purpose was to evaluate whether they might help to distinguish between RAF and Iraqi Hunters during Operation *Vantage*, the British effort to support Kuwait during the Iraq-Kuwait Crisis of 1961. In the event they were not required as the crisis ended before the experiments reached a conclusion.

**Hunter FR.10, XF428 'C', 4 (AC) Sqn, RAF Gütersloh, c1962** | Seen in standard camouflage scheme, XF428 displays 4 Sqn's distinctive markings that allude to the unit's early use of the wireless for artillery co-operation. XF428 was the recipient of a number of 'zaps', the badge of 306 Sqn Royal Netherlands Air Force being prominent on the fin, while an Iron Cross and a cartoon 'Snoopy' flying, it seems, a Republic RF-84F Thunderflash appear forward of the engine intake. It is assumed these were applied during a joint RAF/NATO photo-recon exercise. 306 Squadron RNLAF is a reconnaissance unit and both Germany and the Netherlands operated RF-84Fs.

**Hunter FR.10, XF457 'T', 2 (AC) Sqn, RAF Jever, 1968** | Delivered as an FR.10 to 2 Sqn in January 1961, the unit's prominent white triangles on a black bar on the rear fuselage is repeated in miniature on the black nosewheel door along with the aircraft's individual letter in white. The colour scheme is the standard disruptive camouflage pattern with LAG undersides.

**Hunter T.7, XL601, 1 Sqn, RAF Stradishall, 1959** | XL601 was a new-build T.7 which ultimately went on the serve with the Harrier Conversion Unit (as did XL596 below), 4 FTS, 237 OCU, the FAA and FRADU. XL601 is shown in overall HSS with the yellow wing and fuselage bands favoured for trainers in the late 1950s and early 1960s. 1 Squadron's markings are displayed on the nose and, to ensure there is absolutely no doubt as to the rightful owners, 'No I(F) Squadron' is painted in black on the 100-gallon drop tanks.

**Hunter T.7, XL564 '99', 229 OCU (63 Sqn), RAF Chivenor, 1968** | Following its first flight in January 1958, XL564 was issued to the A&AEE at Boscombe Down and used for trials work including UHF radio evaluation. Later it was used extensively by the ETPS in the so-called 'Raspberry Ripple' colour scheme but was unfortunately lost in August 1998 at Boscombe Down as a result of a throttle restriction. Information on XL564's movements between these two periods is scarce and patchy, but a photo showing the aircraft with 229 OCU in 1968 exists and forms the basis of this illustration. Note the revised day-glo scheme utilising adhesive vinyl stripes rather than painted areas and the 63 Sqn markings on the nose. Unusually XL564 appears to have retained HSS paintwork when most would have been repainted in LAG by this date.

**Hunter T.7, XL596 '1', Harrier Conversion Unit, RAF Wittering, 1970** | XL596, one of two T.7s operated by the Harrier Conversion Unit, is shown here in the HSS and day-glo training aircraft scheme introduced in the mid-1960s. Visibility was improved over the previous scheme but the day-glo paint was very prone to fading. As a result a modified version using strips of adhesive day-glo coloured vinyl was introduced (see illustration of XL564). The photo on which this illustration is based shows significant fading to the day-glo on the top of the nose and undersides.

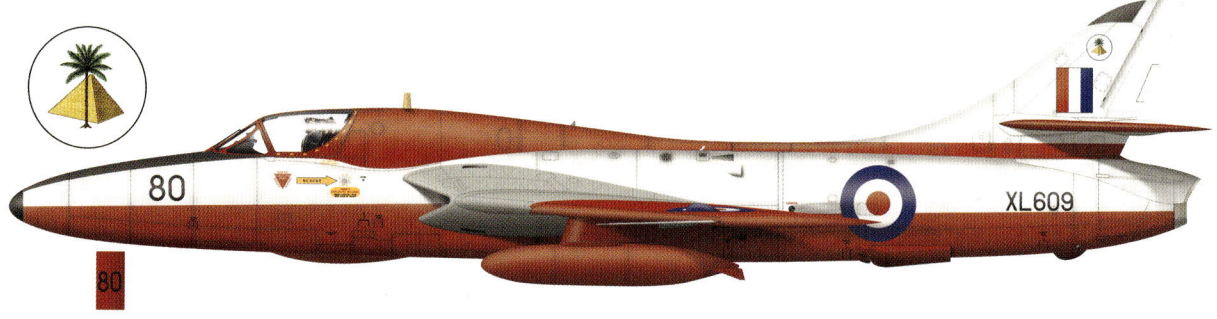

**Hunter T.7, XL609 '80', 4 Flying Training School, RAF Valley, 1973** | XL609 was due to be converted to T.7A standard in April 1965 but the contract was cancelled and the aircraft was returned to the RAF and 4 FTS. XL609 is illustrated in the training scheme of red and white with LAG inner wing areas which superseded the troublesome day-glo scheme described for XL596 and XL564 above. The 4 FTS pyramid and palm tree emblem is displayed on the fin with the individual code located on the nose and repeated on the nosewheel door.

**T.7 XL596 '1', Harrier Conversion Unit, RAF Wittering, 1970** | These views of XL596 show the coloured panels applied to the wings as part of the colour scheme adopted for all training aircraft by the RAF in the mid-1960s. Note the fading present in the nose and tail day-glo areas; a common occurrence with this type of paint that likely contributed to the demise of the scheme in the early 1970s.

**Hunter T.7 XL619 '77', 45 Sqn, RAF Wittering, 1975** | Having been delivered to 45 Squadron in September 1972, XL619 gained an arrester hook sometime between September 1974 and August 1975. As previously mentioned, it was not unknown for T.7 and T.8 rear fuselages to be swapped and fitted to the 'wrong' Mark during servicing or repair work – resulting in some T.7s becoming 'hookers'. XL619 is illustrated as it appeared at Wittering in August 1975 with what appears to be a replacement fin in primer.

**Hunter T.7, XL613 '613', 237 OCU, RAF Lossiemouth, 1988** | With no Buccaneer trainer available, a few two-seat Hunters were modified to receive the Buccaneer Integrated Flight Instrument System in the left-hand seat position to allow pilots to convert to the 'Bucc'. XL613 is shown in a DG/DSG wrap-around camouflage scheme and displays the OCU's 'swords and mortarboard' emblem on a red disc. Note the low visibility national markings and white rubberised coating on the intake lips and internal surfaces. Although 237 OCU disbanded in October 1991, the RAF's last Hunters soldiered on with 208 Squadron (the last RAF Buccaneer unit) until March 1994.

**Hunter GA.11, WT809 '696/LM', 764 Naval Air Squadron, RNAS Lossiemouth, 1965** | Converted to a GA.11 for the Fleet Air Arm by 1963, WT809 subsequently arrived at RNAS Lossiemouth where it joined 738 NAS. A move to Brawdy then back to Lossiemouth saw WT809 issued to 764 NAS and given the code '696' as seen here. WT809 is shown in the FAA scheme of the mid-1960s with Extra Dark Sea Grey (EDSG) upper surfaces with White undersides and spine. The attractive green and white checks and the scales from the 764 NAS badge is presented on the nose.

**Hunter PR.11, WT723 '866/VL', FRADU, RNAS Yeovilton, 1988** | Converted to a GA.11, WT723 was delivered to the FAA in August 1962 and in December 1964 was further converted to PR.11 standard (receiving the same 3-camera nose used on the FR.10). Following an overhaul and transfer to the FRADU at RNAS Yeovilton in 1973, WT723 served for a further 20 years before being grounded and sent to the School of Aircraft Handling (later the School of Flight Deck Operations) at RNAS Culdrose where it was maintained in serviceable condition until withdrawn in 1996. By the mid-1980s many FRADU Hunters had been repainted in overall DSG as seen here. Of interest is the white/cream protective rubber coating applied to the intake trunking that extends around the intake lips; low visibility red/blue national markings on the wings and fuselage, and the anti-collision light on the spine.

HAWKER HUNTER IN COLOUR 79

**Hunter F.1 WW605, Royal Aircraft Establishment Farnborough, 1954** | The precise history of WW605 is vague but it was operated by 233 OCU at RAF Pembrey and by the RAE, probably at Farnborough, for de-icing trials work. Surviving photographs seem to show external ducting installed to capture warm air from the cold air unit's exhaust in the centre fuselage, routing it into the nose via the destructor access hatch. It appears that air was then distributed to the windscreen via nozzles mounted on the top of the nose. It may also have been used to heat other areas such as the gun pack. During the trials, the aircraft had the nose, tail and outer wing areas of its standard DG/DSG/HSS camouflage scheme overpainted with a high visibility colour, probably orange or yellow.

**Hunter F.4 WV325, Royal Radar Establishment, Pershore, c1955** | The RRE was formed in 1953 following the merger of the Air Ministry's Telecommunications Research Establishment and the British Army's Radar Research and Development Establishment. This government establishment was involved with the development and testing of airborne radar systems and operated a variety of aircraft types at different times. Among these was WV325 which carried the standard DG/DSG/HSS camouflage scheme of the period with national markings in all standard positions. Unusually however, the serial number was repeated, in the same 8-inch-high format as the tail, on the nose below the windscreen.

**Hunter F.4 WT703, c1954** | WT703 spent its entire 10-year service life as a trial's aircraft with Hawker and the A&AEE. Several underwing bombs, RPs and fuel tanks were tested on WT703, including service acceptance trials of the Mk.12 Type 3 aircraft rocket launcher and RP installation most frequently seen on the FGA.9. WT703 is shown carrying a 500lb bomb on the inner pylon and a 100-gallon finless drop tank on the outer. At this time WT703 was mostly flown in primer with just the bare minimum of safety-related stencils applied. A repeat of the serial number was stencilled in white on the nosewheel door, the background of which seems likely to be red, although it is not certain.

**Hunter T.7, WV383, RAE Avionics Flight, early 1970s** | Built as an F.4, WV383 was converted to T.7 standard and returned to the RAF in July 1959. Following service with several squadrons, WV383 was later transferred to the RAE and in the early 1970s was operated by the RAE's Avionics Flight in the colour scheme illustrated here, overall LAG, with an Aircraft Blue fin, wing tips and nose stripe. Compared to other Hunters, WV383's wing roundels were positioned a little further outboard than was typical which resulted in the 'tricolour' effect seen on the outboard ERU breech covers. The RAE's badge and 'Avionics Flight' title are presented on the spine aft of the hood.

**T.8C WT722 '873', FRADU, RNAS Yeovilton, 1980** | Built as an F.4, WT722 was converted to T.8C standard and delivered to 703 NAS in April 1959. Further moves to 764 NAS, 759 NAS and the Air Direction Training Unit at Yeovilton followed. It was while serving with ADTU that a Harley light was fitted in May 1972. WT722 transferred to FRADU in December 1972 where it remained until retirement in 1995. WT722 is shown here in a somewhat worn condition having received a replacement fin which has yet to be repainted. The standard FAA trainer scheme of the period of day-glo panels over LAG is evident. These illustrations show the attractive training aircraft colour scheme of day-glo and LAG used by FAA/FRADU until the less flamboyant overall DSG scheme was adopted across the Hunter fleet in the mid-1980s.

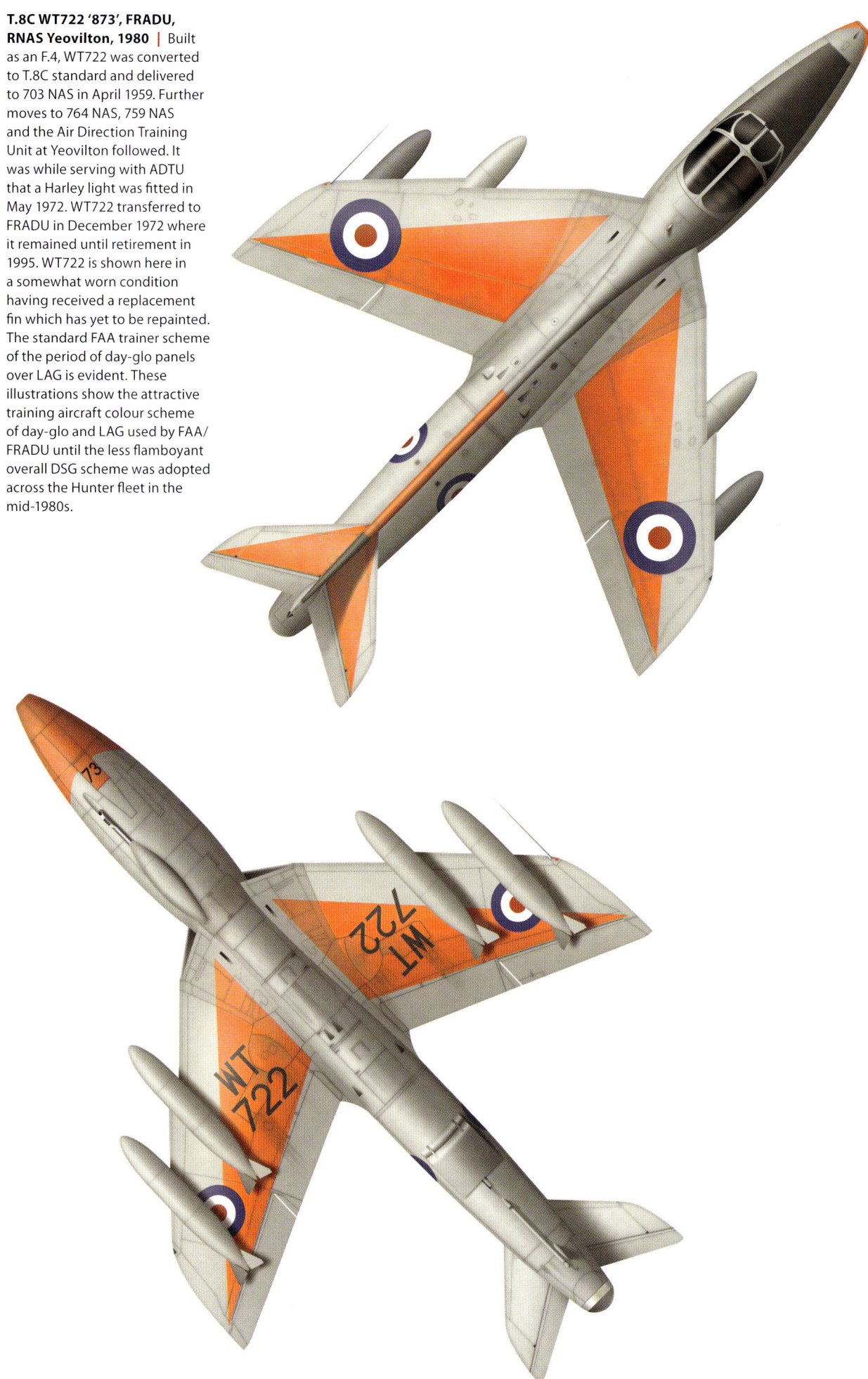

**Hunter T.8, WT722 '873', FRADU, RNAS Yeovilton, 1980**

**Hunter T.8C, XX466 '879/VL', FRADU, RNAS Yeovilton, 1984** | The history of XX466 is an extraordinary one. Built as T.7 XL620 and delivered to the RAF in February 1959, the aircraft was operated by 66 and 74 Squadrons before being struck off charge. After conversion by Hawker to T.70 standard, the aircraft was transferred to Saudi Arabia but was gifted to Jordan in 1968 where it remained until returning to the UK in 1974 in exchange for an FR.10. After overhaul the aircraft gained a new serial, XX466, and entered RAF service for a second time with 229 OCU. With the OCU's transformation into the Tactical Weapons Unit, XX466 then moved to 1 TWU at Brawdy before being taken on by the Royal Navy in 1982. Eight months after being transferred to FRADU in 1984 however, serious degradation of the wing wiring meant that XX466 was withdrawn from flying duties and, in May 1986, moved by road to Culdrose for ground instructional use. During XX466's short time with FRADU it was flown in its, largely unaltered, DG/DSG/LAG colour scheme; only the FAA call-sign (879) and Yeovilton shore code (VL) were added and the fin flash removed – it even retained the TWU badge on the nose!

**Hunter T.8C, WV396 '879/VL', FRADU, RNAS Yeovilton, 1990** | Built as an F.4 and converted to T.8C standard in 1964, WV396 operated with a number of FAA units until placed in storage in 1972. After eight years in store, it was returned to flight with British Aerospace who used WV396 for radio trials before it was allocated to FRADU where it remained until returned to storage at RAF Shawbury in 1995. Shortly after the Falklands War the RN adopted a toned-down colour scheme for their Hunter fleet and, in 1986, WV396 was repainted in overall DSG, the monotony only being broken by the white rubberised coating applied to the engine intakes. Identity numbers and 'Royal Navy' lettering are black and an anti-collision beacon is visible on the spine.

**Hunter T.8M, XL580 '717/VL', 899 NAS, RNAS Yeovilton, 1981** | Delivered in July 1958, XL580 was based at Yeovilton by 1961 and whilst there performed a number of duties including that of 'Admiral's Barge' – the Flag Officer of Flying Training's personal aircraft. Acquired by British Aerospace in late 1978, XL580 was converted to T.8M standard for use as a Sea Harrier trainer which involved the installation of Sea Harrier instrumentation and Ferranti Blue Fox radar. XL580 is illustrated here soon after arriving with 899 NAS (the '717' call-sign was later changed to '719') and features the FAA's EDSG over White colour scheme. 899's 'winged fist' insignia appears on the fin with Yeovilton's 'VL' code. In common with FAA practice, the last two digits of the call-sign are repeated on the nosewheel door.

# Modelling the Hawker Hunter

**Hunter FGA.9, XE552 'D' of 8/43 Sqn, Kormahksar, Aden 1966** | Model is the Revell 1/144 tooling with RetroKit cockpit and replacement vacform canopy. This tooling is now available from Mark 1 models. *Model by Huw Morgan/SIG144*

**Hunter T.7, XL579 '92' of 229 OCU/234 Sqn, Chivenor 1960s** | Model is Whirlybird 1/144 resin which also comes with etched brass, vacformed canopy and excellent decals. The model is based on the Revell tooling. Two-seat Hunters can also be produced by conversion (Retrokit) and now a new injection moulded kit from Mark 1 Models. All are based on, or compatible with, the Revell tooling and all the available aftermarket details. *Model by Mike Verier/SIG144*

**Hunter F.1, WW604 'F' of 233 OCU** | Converted from the 1/72nd Revell F.6 using an Aeroclub tailcone. Mainwheels are from the Airfix FGA.9 and the nose leg was extended by 1mm to give the model the correct 'sit'. The serials are home printed and the yellow 'F' came from the spare decal box. *Model by Mark Gauntlett*

**Hunter F.6, XF462 of 66 Squadron, RAF Acklington, late 1950s** | Made from the 1/72nd Revell F.6, using kit decals, but with the addition of a Squadron Leader's pennant to represent Sqn Ldr Peter Bairsto's personal aircraft. *Model by Ray Ball*

**Hunter F.5, WP197 'O' of 34 Squadron, Nicosia, Cyprus, Suez Crisis October/November 1956** | Academy kit with Heritage Aviation resin wings without the leading edge extensions, and finished sporting the hastily applied yellow and black 'Suez' recognition stripes. *Model by Neil Robinson*

MODELLING THE HAWKER HUNTER  85

**Hunter F.4, WV269 'H' of 74 Sqn** | Academy kit with scratchbuilt converted wings and Aeroclub details.
*Model by Andy Scott*

**Hunter F.5, WN979 'E' of 56 Sqn** | Made from the Aeroclub multi-medium resin and vacform kit.
*Model by Andy Scott*

**Hunter FR.10, XE628 'U' of 4 Sqn** | The Academy kit with Aeroclub upgrade set and home-made FR.10 conversion. The port camera was mounted facing directly to the side, parallel to the horizon, whereas the starboard camera was angled downwards slightly.
*Model by Andy Scott*

**T.7 XL568 'X' 74 Sqn** | Made from the Academy kit with Aeroclub twin-seater conversion set.
*Model by Andy Scott*

# Hawker Hunter Cockpits

**Top:** Hunter F.4 cockpit incorporating all underwing stores and armament modifications. As a result of these upgrades a number of additional panels were fitted to the Hunter's cockpit. These consisted of a panel to the rear of the throttle, immediately aft of the radio controllers, containing bomb fusing and drop tank jettison switches, and a panel to the left of the gunsight containing RP (Rocket Projectile) control switches and an emergency "Clear A/C" button. This F.4 cockpit layout is almost identical to the early F.6, the only significant differences were related to the change from the 100-series to the 200-series Rolls-Royce Avon engine. Specifically, the change to the High-Pressure Fuel Cock control (see the F.4 port shelf photo for details) and the different design of starter button in the centre 'knee' console.

**Centre:** Of particular interest on the port cockpit shelf of the F.4 is the High-Pressure Fuel Cock and the throttle lever with the thumb-operated airbrake in/out switch embedded in its end. The HP Fuel Cock is a valve that allows fuel to flow between the fuel pumps and the engine and, in Hunters with the 100-series Avon engine, is operated by a lever immediately next to the seat – visible in the centre of this photo with the relight button set into the end of its handle. This is a significant cockpit recognition feature as in 200-series engined aircraft this lever is absent and the HP Fuel Cock is operated by the first 2in of movement of the throttle lever; a spring-loaded catch preventing the HP Fuel Cock from being inadvertently shut off when the throttle lever is pulled back to idle.

**Bottom:** A prominent feature of the Hunter's cockpit is the Ferranti Mk.5 gyro gunsight (GGS). In the case of fighters up to, and including, the F.6 this was mounted on the electrically retractable Type 7 mount allowing the sight to be lowered away from the pilot when not required reducing crash and ejection hazards. Although this arrangement had previously been used on fighters such as the Meteor, it had a number of disadvantages including marked harmonisation changes due to play in the mechanism exacerbated by the heavy jarring of the sight as it reached the limit of its travel, reduced forward visibility when extended due to the bulky mechanism, and serviceability and weight concerns. As a result, trials of a fixed mounting were conducted aimed at addressing these issues – see the FGA.9 cockpit for further details. Note the E2 emergency compass and the fire warning light/extinguisher button on the panel to the right of the GGS. Note also the gunsight cine camera mounted on top of the GGS. This recorded the same view as seen by the pilot through the sight and was in addition to the G45 (or G90 in later aircraft) gun camera mounted in the aircraft's nose. Visible on the starboard cockpit shelf are the oxygen regulator, fuel gauge/control panel and Rebecca 7 navigation system control unit.

**Top:** The Hunter's cockpit, compact at the best of times, became ever more cluttered as time went on and modifications and upgrades were incorporated. Here we have the cockpit of XE601, modified to full FGA.9 standard. Of particular note are the armament control switches which have now, mostly, been collected together on the panel to the left of the gunsight. The sight itself is now the Ferranti Mk.8 GGS mounted on a non-retractable fixed mounting. This fixed mount, constructed from a light alloy forging, was designed by the Royal Aircraft Establishment and trialled by the CFE and A&AEE in F.1 WT599 at Dunsfold in late 1954. As well as addressing the concerns described in the F.4 cockpit caption, the fixed mount allowed the whole area above the instrument panel to be 'decked in' preventing reflections from the back of the instrument panel from reaching the windscreen. To the right of the GGS is a large red-painted 'plug'. This is the Master Armament Safety Break (MASB) which, once removed from its stowed position and plugged into the socket visible in front of it, connects power to the gun and RP firing and bomb release circuits. Prior to the FGA.9, the MASB was located in the port wheel well and was connected by a ground crewman at a taxi holding point – the pilot holding both hands visibly clear of the cockpit while he did so. Also note the brake 'chute streaming switch (shaped like a parachute) and red "stream" indicator at the far left of the instrument panel coaming, below the stopwatch holder. Turning our attention to the control column, it will be noticed that a white 'arrowhead' is painted on the very top of the stick. Notice also a white painted disc, the bottom half of which is just visible below the gunsight between the airspeed indicator and artificial horizon. The Hunter was a very spin resistant aircraft but, if a spin did develop, standard recovery procedure involved positively centralising the rudder and ailerons and moving the stick progressively forward until the spin stopped. These white painted marks provided a simple datum for keeping the ailerons centralised during the procedure.

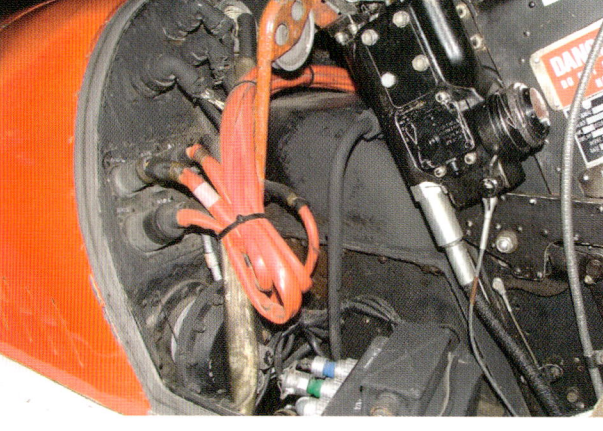

**Above:** Almost every available nook and cranny of the FGA.9 cockpit was used to accommodate the additional controls, instruments and indicators required for the mark. This image illustrates some of these additional panels and the often 'interesting' places they were located. At the top centre of the photo is the gun control panel (with three toggle switches); a feature first introduced on the FGA.9. This allowed pairs of guns (outboard or inboard) or all four Aden cannon to be selected for firing. This selection was not possible on earlier Marks and introduced an additional degree of flexibility to the, now primarily, ground-attack Hunter. Below the gun switches is a panel containing a variety of switches and indicators for cockpit lighting and the IFF and engine anti-icing systems. Below that is the seemingly 'desperate for space' IFF/SSR control unit mounted on an angled bracket which almost entirely obscures the oxygen regulator from the pilot's view. It also meant the instrument panel dimmer switches, which had been happily resident in this location since the F.1, were evicted to a narrow panel wedged between the seat and starboard shelf!

**Above right:** The more sophisticated avionics of the later Hunters necessitated a significant increase in the amount of wiring in the aircraft. The bulkhead behind the seat headbox was, in early Hunters, relatively devoid of detail but, latterly, provided a route into the cockpit for the cabling connecting controls and instrumentation never envisaged when the Hunter first entered service. As a result, this area in the FGA.9 is bristling with electrical connections and bundled wiring looms. Note how the bare aluminium connectors were, often crudely, painted with matt black paint to reduce reflections in the canopy. Also of interest in this image are the BTRU (Barostatic Time Release Unit) on the side of the headbox, which automatically released the pilot's seat harness below 10,000ft after ejection, and the pulley with red-painted guide which routed the cable triggering the hood jettison unit.

**Top:** The Martin Baker Mk.2H ejection seat as fitted to the majority of single-seat RAF Hunters. The seat is fully automated and, once ejection has been initiated using either the seat pan or top handles, will automatically release the seat harness, separate the pilot from the seat and deploy his parachute below 10,000ft. Note the separate seat and parachute harnesses, the khaki coloured equipment being the parachute, backpad and harness, and the blue straps being the seat harness. Note also the thinner blue leg lines which, in conjunction with garters worn as part of the flying kit, drew the pilot's legs close to the seat pan during ejection. The Mk.3H seat, sometimes fitted to late F.6 and FGA.9 aircraft is very similar, the most significant difference being the lack of thigh guards and the relocation of the emergency oxygen bottle, just visible mounted on the rear of the seat, to the front of the seat pan. Hunter trainers were fitted with Mk.4H seats; a more sophisticated, lightweight model with an integrated seat and parachute harness.

**Bottom left:** The instrument panel of the T.7 trainer. Notice how the pupil's side of the panel (left side) was designed to mimic as closely as possible the layout of the single seater aircraft, with an almost identical main panel in front of the student, port side panel (only the edge of which is visible in this image) and the armament panel to the left of the Mk.8 gunsight. The T.7 cockpit did not feature the same side shelves as the single seaters so the fuel panel, retaining the same basic layout, was moved to the centre of the trainer's panel instead. Below that, the oxygen regulator and Rebecca control unit were mounted. The instructor's panel contained a simplified set of flight instruments including an artificial horizon and repeater compass. With reference to the white painted disc (to aid in spin recovery) described in the FGA.9 cockpit photo, you will note the same disc duplicated on each side of the trainer cockpit. On the student's side there is nowhere convenient to paint the disc, the area being cluttered with dimmer switches and indicators, so a separate metal bracket shaped like a lollipop was fitted immediately below the port gunsight instead. *Tony Buttler collection*

**Bottom right:** A perfect example of the longevity and versatility of the Hunter airframe is XF995. Built as an F.4 and first flown in 1956, XF995 was operated by 247 Squadron and 229 OCU before being converted to a T.8B for the Fleet Air Arm in 1963. The aircraft was later transferred back to the RAF and used by 237 OCU as a conversion trainer for Buccaneer crews. XF995's RAF career ended as an instructional airframe at Cranwell but, over sixty years after being built, is again earning her keep flying with Hawker Hunter Aviation Ltd in a trials support and aerial threat simulation role for the MoD. The cockpit is pictured here while at Cranwell – note the installation of the Buccaneer's Integrated Flight Instrument System (IFIS) in the left-hand seat position. The T.8 differed from the T.7 in that it had an airfield arrester hook fitted for use by the FAA. The T.8B differed from the T.8 in the fitting of IFIS and the TACAN tactical air navigation system; gun and radar ranging were deleted. In addition to four T.8Bs, 237 OCU also operated four T.7s modified with IFIS, designated as T.7A. *Newark Air Museum*

# Appendices

## APPENDIX 1 **ROYAL AIR FORCE HUNTER SQUADRONS**

### NOTES

1) 'Period of use' is that in which Hunters are understood to have been on unit strength and thus formed the operational core of the squadron. However, periods of transition (as a particular Mark or aircraft type was replaced by another) are unavoidably included.

2) Though not specifically mentioned, most Hunter squadrons acquired at least one two-seat Hunter from 1959 – some of which were retained by a parent unit after it had re-equipped with more modern types e.g. the Lightning.

3) Abbreviations used below: 'DB' = disbanded; 'FD' = formed; 'RE' = re-equipped; 'RF' = reformed; 'WFU' = withdrawn from use.

| Sqn or Flight | Mark(s) used | Period used | Comments |
|---|---|---|---|
| 1 Squadron | F.5<br>F.6<br>FGA.9 | 9.1955 – 7.58<br>7.58 – 3.60<br>1.60 – 8.69 | RE 9.55 Tangmere, DB 1.7.58. (F.2, WN919, briefly used by 1 Sqn). RF 2.7.58 Stradishall, 11.61 to Waterbeach, 14.8.63 West Raynham. To Wittering 7.69 with Hunters being replaced by Harrier GR.1s |
| 2 Squadron | FR.10 | 2.61 – 3.71 | Germany based: Hunters replaced the Swift FR.5. 2 Sqn became 2 (Hunter) Sqn in 12.70 when 2 (Phantom) Sqn formed. (FR.10s replaced by Phantom FGR.2) |
| 3 Squadron | F.4 | 6.56 – 6.57 | Germany based: Hunters replaced the Sabre F.4. Unit DB 15.6.57 |
| 4 Squadron (Germany) | F.4<br>F.6<br>(Swift FR.5)<br>FR.10 | 7.55 – 2.57<br>2.57 – 12.60<br>(12.60 – 2.61)<br>12.60 – 5.70 | Hunters replaced Sabres. Sqn DB Jever, Germany 30.12.60. RF Gütersloh 31.12.60 in fighter-recce role (possibly used ex-79 Sqn Swifts briefly). German element of 4 Sqn DB 30.5.70. RF 1.6.70 with Harrier GR.1s at Wildenrath |
| 4 Squadron (UK element) | FGA.9 | 9.69 – 5.70 | Rec'd ex-54 Sqn FGA.9s at West. Raynham. Wittering by 3.70. RE Harrier GR.1 from 4.70. Joined German element 30.9.70 |
| 8 Squadron | FGA.9<br>FR.10<br>FR.10 | 1.60 – 12.71<br>4.61 – 3.63<br>9.67 – 12.71 | Based at Khormaksar, Aden, 10.61. To Bahrain 8.9.67. (FR.10s left to form 1417 Flt 3.63; then reabsorbed [+ 4 x T.7s] by 8 Sqn 8.9.67. Masirah, Oman 8.67. DB Muharraq, Bahrain, 21.12.71 |
| 14 Squadron | F.4<br>F.6 | 5.55 – 5.57<br>4.57 – 12.62 | Germany based: DB 17.12.62 Gütersloh (Sqn RF same day on Canberra B(I).8 by renumbering 88 Sqn) |
| 19 Squadron | F.6 | 10.56 – 2.63 | RE F.6 at Church Fenton. RE Lightning F.2 Leconfield from 12.62 |
| 20 Squadron | F.4<br>F.6 | 11.55 – 6.57<br>5.57 – 12.60 | Germany based: Hunters replaced Sabre F.4s at Oldenburg 11.55. DB Gütersloh 30.12.60 |
| 20 Squadron | FGA.9<br>Pioneer CC.1 | 9.61 – 2.70<br>1.69 – 1.70 | RF Tengah, Singapore. Pioneers added for forward air control duties. DB 2.70. (RF Harrier GR.1, Wildenrath, 12.70) |
| 26 Squadron | F.4<br>F.6 | 6.55 – 9.57<br>6.58 – 12.60 | Replaced Sabres at Oldenburg, Germany. DB 10.9.57 RF Ahlhorn 7.6.58. DB Gütersloh 30.12.60 |
| 28 Squadron | FGA.9 | 5.62 – 2.1.67 | Provided Hong Kong's sole air defence/strike unit. DB 2.1.67 |
| 34 Squadron | F.5 | 10.55 – 1.58 | DB Tangmere 15.1.58 |
| 41 Squadron | F.5 | 6.55 – 1.58 | DB Biggin Hill 31.1.58 |
| 43 Squadron | F.1<br>F.4<br>F.6<br>FGA.9 | 7.54 – 11.56<br>2.56 – 7.58<br>1.58 – 7.60<br>5.60 – 10.67 | Based at Leuchars, Squadron **introduced the type to operational** service. Nicosia 6.61; Khormaksar 1.3.63 and 'Aden Strike Wing'. DB Khormaksar 7.11.67. (NOTE: 43 Sqn briefly operated F.6s in Nov/Dec 1956) |
| 45 Squadron | FGA.9 | 8.72 – 7.76 | RF 1.8.72 at West Raynham as an advanced training unit. Moved to Wittering 9.72. Wittering Hunter Wing formed 2.9.74 to administer 45 & 58 Sqns. 45 Sqn & Wing DB 26.7.76 |

| Squadron | Mark | Dates | Notes |
|---|---|---|---|
| 54 Squadron | F.1<br>F.4<br>F.6<br>FGA.9 | 2.55 – 9.55<br>9.55 – 1.57<br>1.57 – 3.60<br>3.60 – 9.69 | RE 2.55 at Odiham. 7.59 moved to Stradishall, then 11.61 to Waterbeach. 14.8.63 to West Raynham. (Sqn RE with Phantom FGR.2 at Coningsby 9.69, but the FGA.9s remained at West Raynham for 4 Sqn's *UK* Element) |
| 56 Squadron | F.5<br>F.6 | 6.55 – 11.58<br>11.58 – 1.61 | RE 9.55 at Waterbeach. Wattisham 7.59. RE Lightning F.1A, 12.60 (Previously a Meteor F.8 sqn, Swift F.1/F.2s acquired from 2.54 but WFU 3.55. Hunters thus replaced Meteors) |
| 58 Squadron | FGA.9 | 8.73 – 6.76 | RF 8.73 at Wittering from core provided by 45 Sqn. (Part of Wittering Hunter Wing from 2.9.74). DB 4.6.76 |
| 63 Squadron | F.6 | 11.56 – 10.58 | Replaced Meteor F.8s 11.56 at Waterbeach. DB 30.10.58 |
| 65 Squadron | F.6 | 11.56 – 3.61 | Replaced Meteor F.8s from 11.56 at Duxford. DB 31.3.61 |
| 66 Squadron | F.4<br>F.6 | 3.56 – 1.57<br>10.56 – 9.60 | 20+ Sabres replaced by 8 Hunter F.4s in 3.56 at Linton-on-Ouse. 4 x Meteor F.8s rec'd in 1956 to maintain pilot hours were kept until sufficient Hunter F.6s came on line in 10.56. To Acklington 2.57. DB there 30.9.60 |
| 67 Squadron | F.4 | 1.56 – 5.57 | Replaced Sabre F.4s, Brüggen, Germany. DB there 31.5.57 |
| 71 Squadron | F.4 | 4.56 – 5.57 | Replaced Sabre F.4s, Brüggen, Germany. DB there 31.5.57 |
| 74 Squadron | F.4<br>F.6 | 3.57 – 1.58<br>11.57 – 11.60 | Meteor F.8 unit, RE Hunter F.4 at Horsham St Faith. Moved to Coltishall 6.59. (Lightning F.1s received from 6.60.) |
| *79 Squadron* | FR.10 | 12.60 | *Gütersloh based Swift FR.5 unit. DB 30.12.60: it seems unlikely that 79 rec'd any Hunters. See 4 Sqn & 79(R) Sqn* |
| 92 Squadron | F.4<br>F.6 | 4.56 – 3.57<br>3.57 – 4.63 | Replaced Sabre F.4s at Linton-on-Ouse. At Middleton St George by 3.57. RE Lightning F.2, Leconfield, from 4.63 |
| 93 Squadron | F.4<br>F.6 | 1.56 – 3.57<br>3.57 – 12.60 | Replaced Sabre F.4s at Jever. DB there 30.12.60 |
| 98 Squadron | F.4 | 4.55 – 7.57 | Jever-based, replaced Venom FB.1s. DB there 25.7.57 |
| 111 Squadron | F.4<br>F.6 | 6.55 – 11.56<br>11.56 – 8.61 | Replaced Meteor F.8s at North Weald. RE Lightning F.1A at Wattisham from 4.61 |
| 112 Squadron | F.4 | 4.56 – 5.57 | Replaced Sabre F.4s at Brüggen. DB there 31.5.57 |
| 118 Squadron | F.4 | 5.55 – 8.57 | Jever-based, replaced Venom FB.1s. DB there 22.8.57 |
| 130 Squadron | F.4 | 4.56 – 5.57 | Replaced Sabre F.4s at Brüggen. DB there 31.5.57 |
| 208 Squadron | F.5<br>F.6<br>FGA.9 | 1.58 – 2.58<br>2.58 – 3.59<br>3.60 – 9.71 | Detachment rec'd ex-34 Sqn F.5s at Tangmere 1.58. RE F.6s, 2.58. Cyprus 3.58, DB there 3.59. RF Kenya 4.59 (Venoms). RE FGA.9s in 3.60. Khormaksar 11.61: 6.64 to Muharraq, Bahrain. DB there 9.71 |
| 222 Squadron | F.1<br>F.4 | 12.54 – 8.56<br>8.56 – 11.57 | Replaced Meteor F.8s at Leuchars. DB there 1.11.57 |
| 234 Squadron | F.4 | 5.56 – 7.57 | Replaced Sabre F.4s at Geilenkirchen. DB there 15.7.57 |
| 245 Squadron | F.4 | 3.57 – 6.57 | Replaced Meteor F.8s at Stradishall. DB there 30.6.57 |
| 247 Squadron | *F.1*<br>F.4<br>F.6 | <br>5.55 – 4.57<br>3.57 – 12.57 | Odiham based, the unit's expected F.1s went instead to 54 Sqn. However, two F.4s arrived on 16.5.55 and Meteor replacement commenced. DB at Odiham 31.12.57 |
| 257 Squadron | F.2 | 9.54 – 3.57 | Replaced Meteor F.8s at Wattisham. DB there 31.3.57 |
| 263 Squadron | F.2<br>F.5<br>F.6 | 2.55 – 10.56<br>5.55 – 8.56<br>?.56 – 7.58 | Hunter F.2s replaced Meteor F.8s at Wattisham. DB at Stradishall 2.7.58 |
| 1417 Flight | FR.10<br>T.7 | 1.3.63 – 8.6.67<br>1.3.63 – 8.6.67 | Formed from recce element of 8 Sqn at Khormaksar with 4 x FR.10 + Stn Flight's 4 x T.7s. 1417 Flight absorbed by 8 Sqn 8.6.67 |
| Aden Strike Wing | FGA.9, FR.10, T.7 | | Umbrella unit for squadrons/flights operating against insurgents during Aden Emergency 1963 to 1967. |

## APPENDIX 2 PRINCIPAL RAF HUNTER TRAINING UNITS
(Plus select listing of second tier Hunter units)

| Unit | Mark(s) | Period | Comments |
|---|---|---|---|
| 229 OCU | F.1s from 1955. F.4, F.6, F.6A, T.7 (from 8.58), FGA.9. FR.10s also used | (Unit extant 12.50 – 2.9.74) Hunters used 1955 to 1974 (T.7 from 6.58) | Formed at Leuchars by redesignating B & D Flights of 226 OCU. To Chivenor 3.51. Codes ES and RS often used until c1960. 229 OCU applied motifs/colours of 145 & 234 reserve Sqns from 1959. 145's motif shifted to 226 OCU (Lightnings) mid-1963. OCU applied 79 reserve Sqn motif from 2.1.67 to 2.9.74. DB 2.9.74. **Shadow or reserve squadrons? – see Note 1** |
| 229 OCU Weapon Instructor Flight | F.6, F.6A, FGA.9 | 11.65? – 9.1974 | Formed part of 229 OCU after DFCS disbanded. 63 Sqn's colours migrating to 229 OCU |
| 233 OCU (i) | Hunter F.1 | (Unit extant 1.9.52 – 1.9.57) | Vampires initially, joined by Hunter F.1s in 1955 to assist 229 OCU in coping with large numbers of fighter pilots converting to type until 1957 defence review brought such need to a premature end |
| TWU – Tactical Weapons Units | F.6, F.6A, T.7, FGA.9, FR.10<br><br>Hawk T.1 | 2.9.74 – 31.8.92 (Hunters used 1974 – 1984)<br><br>1.78 – 31.8.92 | Formed at Brawdy out of 229 OCU (encompassing 63[R], 79[R] & 234[R] Sqns). TWU became 1 TWU when 2 TWU formed 31.7.78 at Lossiemouth. Hunter training ops ceased by 7.84: some retained as hacks to 9.84 (but XE597 & XE624 retained until 29.4.85) |
| 4 FTS – Flying Training School | F.6, T.7 | RF 15.8.60 Hunters used 1967 to 1979 (or 1980?) | Hunters formed 3 Sqn within 4 FTS supplementing Gnat T.1s at Valley from 1967. Hawks rec'd from 11.1976 |
| Central Fighter Establishment | | 4.9.44 – 1.2.66 | **Please Refer to Note 2** |
| Fighter Weapons School | F.1, F.4, F.6 | 1.1.55 – 7.3.58 | FD Leconfield to train Meteor, Vampire, Venom, Sabre and Hunter pilots in use of guns, bombs and RPs. Absorbed by CFE 7.3.58 |
| 12 Squadron (Buccaneer S.2 unit) | T.7, T.7A, T.8 (used at various times) F.6 (XF383) | 10.69 – 10.93<br><br>4.8.80 – 1.82 | RF 1.10.69 on Buccaneer S.2 at Honington. Two-seat Hunters used throughout but single-seater(s) lent by TWU while S.2 fleet was grounded. 8.80 moved to Lossiemouth. DB 10.93 |
| 15 Squadron (Buccaneer S.2 unit) | T.7, T.7A<br><br>F.6 | 1971 – 1982<br><br>1980 | RF 1.10.70 on Buccaneer S.2 at Honington. Laarbruch by 11.1.71. [In 1980 the Sqn's Hunters were joined for several months by T.8s and 4 x F.6s while S.2 fleet was grounded.] 15 Sqn absorbed into 16 Sqn 1.7.83 |
| 16 Squadron (Buccaneer S.2 unit) | T.7, T.7A | Late 1970s (?) – 1982 | RF 8.1.73 as Buccaneer S.2 unit at Laarbruch. DB as S.2 unit 2.84. *[15 & 16 Sqns could also draw on Laarbruch Stn Flt Hunters. In 1982 all Laarbruch-based Hunters were transferred to the Stn Flight]* |
| 208 Squadron (Buccaneer S.2 unit) | T.7, T.7A, T.8 (used at various times)<br><br>F.6A, FGA.9 | 1974(?) – 3.94<br><br>1980 – 1981(?) | RF 1.7.74 as Buccaneer S.2 unit, Honington. [Single-seat Hunters rec'd while S.2 fleet remained grounded 1980-81.] Moved to Lossiemouth 1.7.83 and DB there 31.3.94.<br>**Buccaneer Training Flight** formed within 208 Sqn to continue training task after 237 OCU disbanded using T.8C XF967 among others. BT Flight disbanded late 1992 |
| 216 Squadron (Buccaneer S.2 unit) | T.7, T.7A<br><br>F.6 (XF383) | 7.79 – 8.80<br><br>7.80 – 8.80 | RF 1.7.79 as Buccaneer S.2 unit at Honington. To Lossiemouth 4.7.80 & rec'd F.6. Absorbed by 12 Sqn on 4.8.80 |
| 237 OCU (Buccaneer S.2 unit) | Hunter T.7, T.7A, T.8 F.6A temporarily | (Unit extant 3.71 – 10.91) | RF Honington 1.3.71 as 237 (Buccaneer) OCU. DB 1.10.91. Hunter fleet expanded when Buccaneers were grounded. DB Lossiemouth 1.10.91 |
| Harrier Conversion Team/Harrier Conversion Unit | Harrier GR.1, T.2 Hunter FGA.9, T.7 | 1.1.69 – 1.10.70 | Formed at Wittering. Renamed Harrier Conversion Unit 1.4.70. Became 233 OCU Wittering, 1.10.70 |

| | | | |
|---|---|---|---|
| 233 OCU **(ii)** | Harrier GR.1<br>Hunter FGA.9, T.7 | RF 1.10.70 | OCU formed from Harrier Conversion Unit. Hunters used as chase planes by instructors until sufficient Harrier T.2s arrived |
| RAF Wittering Hunter Wing | FGA.9, T.7 | 2.9.74 –<br>26.7.76 | Formed to administer 45 and 58 Sqns at Wittering. DB 26.7.76. |

## NOTE 1
**'Shadow' or 'Reserve'**, which is correct – one or both?

The term shadow squadron or reserve squadron has been used repeatedly, usually in the same context, to describe the same thing, both having long since been used by observers as fully-interchangeable alternatives without any apparent contradiction. But were they the same?

In 1954, as Cold War tensions increased, consideration was given to raising additional fighter squadrons from within selected training establishments to strengthen Fighter Command during the initial stages of an actual war. RAF training establishments were already expected to provide reinforcements of instructors and aircraft, either individually or in small groups, to existing front-line units anyway but the creation, on paper at least, of entire (albeit transitory) squadrons that *might* be activated during the initial phases of a national crisis represented a further reinforcement option. (This concept naturally appealed to HM Exchequer given that it was only envisaged as a contingency: ergo, unless war actually did break out costs would remain minimal because the 'squadrons' should never need to exist at all.)

In 1956, as the concept grew, a handful of redundant squadron number plates were promulgated and listed as 'shadow squadrons', but in 1957/58 the term was officially changed to 'reserve squadrons' with number plates allocated to the appropriate units in readiness for the crisis when it arose. Of course, the original intention remained – reserve squadrons were to exist on paper *only*, until, or indeed *if*, they were ordered to mobilise.

The directive was soon disregarded of course, but which unit became the first to exhibit their reserve colours remains unknown to the authors, although a favourite must be 229 OCU which, if not the first, was certainly among them given that several of their Hunters were wearing 145 or 234 Squadron marks by early 1959.

Years later, most remaining Hunter-equipped *reserve* squadrons had the suffix [R] appended to their number plates, namely: 63 which became 63[Reserve] Sqn; 79 became 79[R] and 234 became 234[R] Sqn – all on 2.9.1974. However, 145 reserve Sqn, which relinquished Hunters on 1.6.63, never did receive an 'R' suffix (not even as a Lightning unit within 226 OCU from 1963 to 1970).

To this author (MD) it seems pretty clear that beyond 1957 the word 'shadow' was officially replaced by 'reserve'. It seems likely too that the seat of confusion lies with the introduction of Reserve squadrons to the RAF at large from mid-1970 and the subsequent application of the suffix R to specific units, presumably as a device to keep well-known yet fast disappearing squadron number plates 'alive' as HMG forced the RAF to continue a policy of relentless decline.

## NOTE 2
**Central Fighter Establishment (CFE)**

Formed on 4.9.44, the CFE's role was to develop and evaluate the latest fighter tactics – consequently it hosted a plethora of specialised sub-units over its near 22-year lifespan, some of which were equipped with Hunters, including:

**Air Fighting Development Squadron** (AFDS) formed on 1.10.44 and received the unit's first Hunter, an F.1, in 7.54, followed thereafter by every RAF Hunter variant excepting the FR.10.

**Day Fighter Leaders School** (DFLS) formed on 27.12.44, its title changing to Day Fighter Leaders *Squadron* in 4.1956. It then became the **Day Fighter Combat Squadron** (DFCS) on 15.3.1958 when it and other sub-units were encompassed by the 'parent' **Fighter Combat School** (FCS). This arrangement lasted until 1.7.62 when the FCS divided to create the **Day Fighter Combat School** and the Javelin OCS. The DFCS disbanded on 1.11.65, on which date (or shortly thereafter) it was re-established within 229 OCU as the Weapon Instructor Flight.

**Fighter Command Trials Unit** (FCTU) When the CFE disbanded on 1.2.66 the AFDS was redesignated FCTU by which point just two Hunter F.6s remained on charge in addition to its Lightning F.6s. The FCTU disbanded on 30.6.67.

**Instrument Rating Squadron** (Instrument Rating Flight prior to 1960) was also a component of the CFE.

## APPENDIX 3 ROYAL NAVY HUNTER-EQUIPPED FAA SQUADRONS AND CIVILIAN-RUN UNITS

| Unit | Mark(s) | Period of use | Comments |
| --- | --- | --- | --- |
| 700 B NAS | T.8 | 4.65 – 5.65 | FD Lossiemouth 9.4.65; DB there 30.9.65. Buccaneer S.2 used to 30.9.65 |
| 700 Y NAS | T.8 | 11.58 – 1.59 | FD Yeovilton 4.11.58; RF 1.7.59 as 892 NAS on Sea Vixen FAW.1 |
| 700 Z NAS | T.8<br>T.8B | 5.61 – 7.61<br>7.61 – 12.62 | FD Lossiemouth 7.3.61; also used Buccaneer S.1, Meteor T.7 and Sea Prince. RF as 809 NAS 15.1.63 |
| 736 NAS | T.8 | 7.58 – 11.58 | Several other types also in use. Sqn provided advanced training and training of Air Warfare Instructors at this time |
| 738 NAS | T.8/T.8C<br>GA.11 | 6.62 – 5.70<br>6.62 – 5.70 | Advanced training squadron: duties included low-level navigation, ground attack and air-to-air weapons training. DB 8.5.70 |
| 759 NAS | T.8/T.8C | 7.63 – 12.69 | RF Brawdy 1.8.63 as the Naval Advanced Flying Training School. DB 24.12.69 at Brawdy |
| 764 NAS | T.8/T.8C/T.8C<br>GA.11/PR.11 | 7.58 – 7.72<br>7.62 – 7.72 | RE Lossiemouth. By 3.59 its prime role was air warfare instructor training. T.8Bs arrived in 1968, T.8Cs later. DB Lossiemouth 27.7.72 |
| 803 NAS | T.8 | 5.60 – 7.60 | T.8, XF357, used while Squadron was shore based at Lossiemouth |
| 899 NAS | T.8M | 8.81 – 10.93 | 899 NAS Operational Evaluation Unit |
| RN civilian-run units | T.8, GA.11, PR.11 | | **Please refer to Note 1 for general explanation.** |

### NOTE 1
Apart from its use with the Royal Navy's regular Fleet Air Arm squadrons, Hunters were also used by RN-administered civilian operated flying units as listed below:

**Airwork Ltd:** Civilian-run, this unit commenced work in 1.50, at Brawdy, to provide aircraft for cooperation with RN units. Moving to Yeovilton in 1.61, it operated as the **Air Direction Training Unit**. ADTU later merged into the **Fleet Requirements and Air Direction Training Unit** (FRADU) on 1.12.72 (the word 'Training' being subsequently dropped).

**Fleet Requirements Unit** (FRU): Run by Airwork Ltd, Airwork FRU opened at Hurn on 1.9.52 to supply some, later all, of the RN's fleet requirement needs. Moving to Yeovilton on 16.10.72, it was merged into FRADU on 1.12.72.

**FRADU:** Civilian-operated, formed 1.12.72 at Yeovilton to combine the functions of ADTU and FRU. Having received half-a-dozen Hawk T.1s (including T.1As?) between April and December 1994, and with a prediction that additional Hawks would soon be made available, it was decided that the unit's last four Hunters would be retired somewhat prematurely in May 1995. FRADU disbanded on 6 June 2013.

### NOTE 2
In addition to its own T.8 series Hunters, the RN also received at least nine ex-RAF T.7s – at least two of which were/became non-flying instructional airframes only.

# APPENDIX 4 **HUNTER SERIAL NUMBERS** (UK SERVICE ONLY)

**Prototypes**

WB188, WB195, WB202 (Sapphire engined prototype)

**Hunter F.1**

WT555-WT595, WT611-WT660, WT679-WT700, WW599-WW610, WW632-WW645.

**Hunter F.2**

WN888-WN921, WN943-WN953.

**Hunter Mark 3**

Prototype WB188 was converted to become the sole Hunter Mark 3.

**Hunter F.4**

WT701-WT723, WT734-WT780, WT795-WT811, WV253-WV281, WV314-WV334, WV363-WV412, WW589-WW591, WW646-665, XE657-XE689, XE702-XE718, XF289-XF324, XF357-XF370, XF932-XF953, XF967-XF999, XG341, XG342.

**Hunter F.5**

WN954-WN992, WP101-WP150, WP179-WP194.

**Hunter F.6**

WW592-WW598, XE526-XE561, XE579-XE628, XE643-XE656, XF373-XF389, XF414-XF463, XF495-XF527, XF833 (prototype F.6) XG127-XG137, XG150-XG172, XG185-XG211, XG225-XG239, XG251-XG274, XG289-XG298, XJ632-XJ646, XJ673-XJ695, XJ712-XJ718, XK136-XK142, XK149-151

**Hunter T.7**

Hawker private venture prototypes = XJ615 and XJ627.
New-build = XL563-XL579, XL583, XL586, XL587, XL591-XL597, XL600, XL601, XL605, XL609-XL623. (XL605 & XL620 sold to Saudi Arabia 1966: subsequently returned, they re-entered RAF service as XX467 and XX466 respectively).
Known F.4 to T.7 conversions are WV253, WV318, WV372, WV383, XF310 and XF321.

**Hunter T.7A**

Four new-build T.7s, XL568, XL611, XL614, XL616 were upgraded to T.7A standard following the installation of TACAN (TACtical Air Navigation). WV318 became the fifth T.7A, although some sources have referred to it as 'the' T.7B. Usefully, all five received IFIS, a servo-assisted integrated flight instrumentation system as used on newer combat aircraft, including the Buccaneer S.2.

**Hunter T.8**

New-build = XL580-XL582, XL584, XL585, XL598, XL599, XL602-XL604. Ordered as T.7s for the RAF, they were instead diverted to RN control. Additionally, thirty-one F.4s were converted to T.8, T.8B or T.8C standard as required. The T.8B had TACAN and IFIS installed in lieu of the gun while the T.8C received TACAN only (but retained the gun).

**Hunter T.8M**

XL580, XL602 and XL603 were fitted with Blue Fox radar both for the trials of, and later the training of Sea Harrier FRS.1 pilots. The gun was removed.

**Hunter FGA.9 (F.6A and 'Interim' FGA.9)**

128 Hunter F.6s were scheduled for upgrade to FGA.9 standard from 1959, thirty-six of which emerged as the 'Interim' FGA.9 though most were later upgraded to full FGA.9 spec. Later, in 1975/76, two dozen F.6s were modified at Brawdy to F.6A standard. Consequently, both the F.6A and 'Interim' FGA.9 almost matched the full FGA.9 spec, except that both retained the F.6's original Avon 203 engine, while the full-spec FGA.9 received the Avon 207.

**Hunter FR.10**

Thirty-three Hunter F.6s were converted to the Fighter Reconnaissance role to become the FR.10.

**Hunter GA.11 (and PR.11)**

Forty surplus ex-RAF F.4s were converted to perform a tactical weapons training role for the Royal Navy designated GA.11. Several later had a Harley light fitted in the tip of the nose to assist with optical tracking, while others received a camera-nose installation and were redesignated as PR.11.

**Hunter Mark 12**

Two-seat Hunter converted from F.6 to FGA.9 to Mk12. XE531's final configuration was similar to a T.7 albeit with a 'big-bore' Avon engine. The only example of its type, it was destroyed on 17 March 1982.

## APPENDIX 5 HUNTER BASIC DATA – RAF & RN

| Mark | First flight | Engine | Span | Length | Comments |
|---|---|---|---|---|---|
| P.1067 | 20.7.51 | Rolls-Royce Avon 103: 6,500 lb st | 33ft 8in (10.25m) | 45ft 10½in (13.98m) | |
| F.1 | 16.5.53 | Rolls-Royce Avon 113: 7,500 lb st | 33ft 8in (10.25m) | 45ft 10½in (13.98m) | RAF single-seat Hunters carried 4 x 30mm Aden (Armament Development ENfield) revolver cannon with approx 480 rounds |
| F.2 | 14.10.53 | Armstrong-Siddeley Sapphire 101: 8,000 lb st | 33ft 8in (10.25m) | 45ft 10½in (13.98m) | |
| Mk.3 | 12.8.53 | Rolls-Royce Avon RA.7R: 9,600 lb st | 33ft 8in (10.25m) | ? | |
| F.4 | 19.10.54 | Avon 113/115 later 121: 7,500 /8,000 lb st | 33ft 8in (10.25m) | 45ft 10½in (13.98m) | Underwing stores could be carried but rarely were. Some F.4s later rec'd leading-edge wing extensions, possibly for use with training units to ensure student pilots were as familiar as possible with the front-line Hunter F.6 units |
| F.5 | 20.10.54 | Armstrong-Siddeley Sapphire 101: 8,000 lb st | 33ft 8in (10.25m) | 45ft 10½in (13.98m) | As with F.4 underwing stores rarely carried |
| F.6 | 23.5.55 | Avon 203: 10,000 lb st | 33ft 8in (10.25m) | 45ft 10½in (13.98m) | Four-pylon Mod.228 wing. F.6A conversions primarily intended for use by TWU |
| T.7 | 8.7.55 | Avon 121A: 7,550 lb st | 33ft 8in (10.25m) | 48ft 10½in (14.9m) | 1 x Aden cannon only. Gun located under starboard nose. Fitted with four-pylon Mod.228 wing |
| T.8 | 3.5.58 | Avon 122: 7,550 lb st | 33ft 8in (10.25m) | 48ft 10½in (14.9m) | For RN. 1 x Aden under starboard nose (not T.8B or T.8M). Fitted with airfield arrester hook and other naval equipment |
| FGA.9 | 3.7.59 | Avon 207: 10,170 lb st | 33ft 8in (10.25m) | 45ft 10½in (13.98m) | 230-gal tanks on inner pylons braced and stressed for combat manoeuvres (applies to F.6A and 'Interim' FGA.9 also) |
| FR.10 | 7.11.59 | Avon 207: 10,170 lb st | 46ft 1in (14.05m) | 45ft 10½in (13.98m) | Virtual FGA.9 standard. Cameras fitted in nose plus other airframe mods to suit FR role |
| GA.11 | 1962 | Avon 121: 8,000 lb st | 33ft 8in (10.25m) | 45ft 10½in (13.98m) | Guns and related gun-laying radar replaced by ballast. Some GA.11s rec'd FR.10-style camera nose to become the PR.11 |

## APPENDIX 6 GLOSSARY

| | |
|---|---|
| A&AEE | Aircraft & Armament Experimental Establishment |
| AFDS | Air Fighting Development Squadron |
| AES | Air Electronics School |
| AFS | Advanced Flying School |
| ADTU | Air Direction Training Unit |
| ANS | Air Navigation School |
| APC | Armament Practice Camp |
| APS | Armament Practice Station |
| AW&NF OCU | All Weather & Night Fighter OCU |
| BAC | British Aircraft Corporation |
| BCCS | Bomber Command Communications Squadron |
| BCDU | Bomber Command Development Unit |
| BTF | Buccaneer Training Flight |
| CAACU | Civilian Anti-Aircraft Co-operation Unit |
| CATCS | Central Air Traffic Control School |
| CF | Communication Flight; often prefixed with location e.g. Aden CF |
| CFE | Central Fighter Establishment |
| CFS | Central Flying School |
| CNCS | Central Navigation and Control School |
| CS | Communication Squadron; often prefixed with location e.g. Aden CS |
| CSDE | Central Servicing Development Establishment |
| CSE | Central Signals Establishment |
| DFCS | Day Fighter Combat Squadron / Day Fighter Combat School |
| DFLS | Day Fighter Leaders School / Day Fighter Leaders Squadron |
| ECM | Electronic Counter Measures |
| ERU | Ejector Release Unit |
| ETPS | Empire Test Pilots School |
| FAA | Fleet Air Arm |
| FCS | Fighter Combat School |
| FCIRS | Fighter Command Instrument Rating Squadron |
| FRU | Fleet Requirements Unit |
| FRADU | Fleet Requirements & Air Direction Unit |
| FTS | Flying Training School |
| HSA | Hawker Siddeley Aviation |
| HSS | High-Speed Silver |
| MoA | Ministry of Aviation |
| MoD(PE) | Ministry of Defence (Procurement Executive) |
| MoS | Ministry of Supply |
| MU | Maintenance Unit |
| NEA | non-effective airframe |
| OCU | Operational Conversion Unit |
| RAE | Royal Aircraft Establishment (Royal Aerospace Establishment from 1 April 1988) |
| RAFC | Royal Air Force College |
| RAFCAW | Royal Air Force College of Air Warfare |
| RAFFC | Royal Air Force Flying College |
| RRE | Radar Research Establishment |
| SOC | struck off charge |
| SoTT | School of Technical Training |
| TACAN | TACtical Air Navigation |
| TAF | Tactical Air Force e.g. 2TAF 2nd Tactical Air Force |
| TMTS | Trade Management Training School (Scampton) |
| TRE | Telecommunications Research Establishment |
| TT | Target Tug |
| TWU | Tactical Weapons Unit |